CALIFORNIA 2.0

AN INDEPENDENT VISION FOR
CALIFORNIA'S ABUNDANT FUTURE

CALIFORNIA 2.0

JON HENDERSON

HOUNDSTOOTH
PRESS

COPYRIGHT © 2026 JON HENDERSON
All rights reserved.

CALIFORNIA 2.0
An Independent Vision for California's Abundant Future

FIRST EDITION

ISBN   978-1-5445-5147-0   *Hardcover*
        978-1-5445-5146-3   *Paperback*
        978-1-5445-5145-6   *Ebook*
        978-1-5445-5169-2   *Audiobook*

CONTENTS

INTRODUCTION 9

PILLAR I: GROW
1. ENDING HOMELESSNESS AND WILDFIRES THROUGH MASS TIMBER 19
2. UNEMPLOYMENT OVERHAUL 27
3. THE PEOPLE'S PORTFOLIO 33
4. CANNABIS 2.0 41
5. BITCOIN 49

PILLAR II: BUILD
6. HOUSING AT THE SPEED OF HENDERSON 59
7. POWER TO THE PEOPLE 67
8. HIGH-SPEED RAIL AND BEYOND 77
9. CLIMATE, RESILIENCE, AND INSURANCE 83
10. PRISON REFORM AND LABOR THAT HEALS 89
11. IMMIGRATION AND LABOR 97

PILLAR III: GOVERN

12. TOUGH LOVE FOR VANDALISM AND SHOPLIFTING 105
13. BLIND TRUSTS OR BUST 115
14. VOTING ON THE BLOCKCHAIN 119
15. GUN POLICY IN A DIGITAL AGE 125

PILLAR IV: INVENT

16. WATER 133
17. ARTIFICIAL INTELLIGENCE 139
18. INNOVATION AND CLIMATE TECH 145

PILLAR V: DEPLOY

19. DMV 2.0 153
20. THE CLASSROOM CRISIS 159
21. CALIFORNIA'S HEALTHCARE CROSSROADS 165
22. A TRUE MERITOCRACY 173

CLOSING 179

INTRODUCTION

CALIFORNIA DREAMING, AMERICAN AWAKENING

I've spent nearly my entire life in California—I was born in Tarzana, raised in Ventura County, and later headed to San Diego for college before building my career in the Bay Area. I attended Grossmont Junior College and San Diego State University (SDSU), where my years were defined by drumming in punk bands and working at Trader Joe's.

School was never designed for how my brain works. Teachers wrote me up as a "social butterfly" who talked too much, but really, I just learned differently. What once frustrated them—my curiosity, energy, and refusal to shrink myself—became my greatest strengths as an adult, fueling my career in college and later in business: building relationships, generating ideas, and leading with vision.

Having a therapist for a mom meant that I grew up self-reflecting more than most kids did. Over the years, I took every personality test she threw my way, and the one that stuck was the Myers-Briggs. I'm an ENFP—"the Champion." That means

I'm fueled by people, creativity, and big visions, but I wrestle with follow-through when things get too rigid or uninspiring. This explains so much: why school frustrated me, why I thrive in dynamic environments, and why I've always been more comfortable building something new than maintaining the status quo. I realized that I needed a career built on people and vision, not rigid, unimaginative, small-scale thinking.

I originally planned to use a small scholarship from McGeorge School of Law after SDSU, but I later discovered my true calling in financial advising.

I've spent the last twenty-five years building a career and a life in the Bay Area, splitting time primarily between San Francisco and Walnut Creek. Along the way, I've owned homes in several counties—including a cherished property in Tuolumne County at Pine Mountain Lake whose airstrip's Federal Aviation Administration (FAA) identifier, E45, later inspired the name of Echo45 Advisors, my independent registered investment advisory firm launched in 2020.

This is where Independence truly comes into play. If I were still working at a bank-owned firm—or any large corporation, for that matter—I wouldn't be writing this book. I wouldn't be free to say what I believe, call out broken systems, or propose bold reforms. The reality is that too many of our best and brightest never even consider leadership because their livelihoods depend on staying quiet. They have bosses. They have shareholders. They have political masters. I don't. Independence is the only reason I can speak plainly. It's the only reason I can tell the truth without hedging. And it's why California deserves leaders who aren't beholden to parties, donors, or corporations—leaders who are free to think, free to innovate, and free to get it right.

FROM CONTEMPT TO RESPECT

I'm a fan of Malcolm Gladwell. In his 2005 book *Blink*, he discusses John Gottman's research on marriages, noting that contempt is the single best predictor of divorce because couples rarely recover from it. Candidly, in my twenty-five years of talking with everyday people, I've never seen more contempt in our politics—and it only gets amplified from behind a keyboard. But I believe that if we can get to work on shared objectives—like ending homelessness and wildfires—then by the time we start notching some wins together, we'll begin to like one another again. We'll begin to learn more about each other's life paths and stories. And that knowledge will inevitably grow into mutual understanding. Whether you're a married couple or neighbors flying different political flags, now more than ever, it's time to put differences aside and focus on what we absolutely, fundamentally agree on.

Independence means rejecting the labels, the echo chambers, and the incentives to divide. It means focusing on what we can actually build together. When we stop shouting across partisan lines and start solving real problems—homelessness, wildfires, housing—something powerful happens. Wins pile up. Trust starts to return. And respect grows where contempt once lived.

Understanding is the bridge from that respect—an honest look at how we talk about politics and identity.

That shared understanding is the only path forward for our country. And California can lead the way—not just in policy but in how we treat human beings at every level.

ON LANGUAGE AND PERSPECTIVE

Throughout this book, I'll refer to red and blue, left and right, liberal and conservative, and occasionally, up and down. Red and blue represent the two major political parties—Republican and Democrat. Left and right describe the echo chambers that too many Americans find themselves in, amplified by social media and cable news. Liberal and conservative, on the other hand, are not opposites—they're values and mindsets that can exist within the same person. I use these terms as descriptors of mindset, not as fixed identities or camps. My father, who identifies as conservative, despises waste in any form. He repurposes everything—from rainwater to scrap materials—an instinct that runs parallel to many of my most liberal friends, who act from the same ethic of resourcefulness and care. We arrive at the same place by different routes.

But the real divide in America today isn't left versus right—it's up versus down. Most of us aren't looking up because we're too busy trying to build better lives, while a small group at the top controls most of the levers of wealth, media, and influence. I believe our challenge isn't to fight each other horizontally but to rise together vertically—to build something stronger, kinder, and more sustainable from the ground up.

This book is about that upward motion: how we first build, then earn trust through shared progress, and only then have the deeper conversations that move us forward as a people.

That progress—and the respect it builds—sets the stage for California 2.0, where Independence replaces partisanship and balance becomes the foundation for everything that follows.

CALIFORNIA 2.0

When most of the country looks at California, they see a "blue state"—the cudgel of the left or even caricatures of socialism and communism. But the truth is more nuanced. California, just like Texas, is more balanced than the national storyline suggests. In 2024, California voters went about 58 percent Democratic and 38 percent Republican, while Texas voters went about 56 percent Republican and 42 percent Democratic. The two are nearly mirror images of each other. That doesn't make California a one-party monolith; it makes it a state of balance and diversity—a state with enough diversity of thought and experience to demand leaders who can govern for everyone, not just one side of the political spectrum.

That balance is not reflected in our politics because of gerrymandering and entrenched partisanship. Too many Californians—especially Republicans—feel that they have no voice here, just as Democrats often feel voiceless in Texas. The result is migration: friends and clients of mine have left California in retirement, not because they dislike our weather, culture, or opportunities, but because they feel shut out of the conversation. That's a sickness in our democracy. When people stop believing they have a voice, they stop investing in their community's future.

POLITICALLY HOMELESS

I often say I feel politically homeless—and I know I'm not alone. At one point in history, running as an independent might have been seen only as a spoiler to the Republicans or Democrats. But today, the parties themselves are so polarized that many people like me feel we stayed where we were, while the parties left us. I hear this from friends and clients, and even in the media: people say they're tired of voting for the lesser of two evils. I feel the same way, and I think it's terrible that we've accepted that as normal. I'm running for Governor to provide a real option for all those politically homeless Californians who are looking for a vision they can be proud to join—one that focuses on getting results, beautifying our state, and bringing California confidently into the next generation.

That's why California 2.0 isn't just a slogan—it's a home for the politically homeless.

INDEPENDENCE AND RESPECT

People are starved for something genuine, something logical, something visionary. For too long, politicians have seemed disingenuous because they are forced to appeal to their donors. It comes off as fake because, effectively, it is. Like actors, they are being paid to play a role—often in conflict with the very people who elected them to represent their interests. That erosion of authenticity is why trust in politics is so low. Independence is the antidote: when you answer only to the people, you don't need a script, and you don't need spin—you can simply speak the truth.

My worldview was shaped by my parents, and the balance of discipline and compassion they embodied has become the foundation of my governing philosophy. My father, a Marine and twenty-five-year veteran of the police department, instilled duty, discipline, and integrity. My mother, an artist and licensed marriage and family therapist, imparted emotional intelligence, compassion, and an appreciation for nuance. Together, they gave me an invaluable gift: a balanced perspective that allows me to see the world as it is and as it could be.

California has defined my identity—as a son, father, husband, business owner, pilot, and more. My love for this state runs deep, even as I regularly defend it against negative portrayals.

The government shouldn't dictate whom you love, how you worship, or which freedoms you responsibly exercise. Instead, the government should function like a fiduciary financial advisor. In my work, I serve about two hundred clients. Politically, I agree with roughly half and disagree with the other half—but that's irrelevant. My role isn't to impose my values; it's to help them achieve their goals. That's how the government should work: as a fiduciary steward, bound to put the public's interest first. Just as I guide clients toward their goals, I believe California's government should serve with that same fiduciary ethic. This is the essence of government that works—objective, accountable, and focused on delivering results.

A BLUEPRINT OF ABUNDANCE

From mass timber construction to blockchain, from wildfire prevention to water recycling, solutions already exist. What's been missing is the political will and competence to deploy them.

If this optimism feels naive, it's only because we've been conditioned by scarcity politics that pit us against each other and tell us nothing can change. I discovered Ezra Klein and Derek Thompson's book *Abundance* while writing this book and decided to frame my work around their core pillars and add my personal inspiration:

- **Grow:** A future-focused economy that works for everyone
- **Build:** Infrastructure and resilience for the next century
- **Govern:** Respect and integrity in how we run our democracy
- **Invent:** Technology and science in the service of humanity
- **Deploy:** A social contract that actually works

Every chapter that follows connects to one of these pillars. This is not theory. It's a master plan, a blueprint, and an invitation to believe again that California can be the frontier of possibility. As a money manager, I view the world through an inflationary and deflationary lens. I've added that perspective to each concept outlined in the book to further anchor the economic sanity I'm proposing.

I wrote this book for anyone who believes that California can—and must—function better. That's why I believe California can lead again by proving to the nation that the government can work—with competence, optimism, and visible results. This starts with Independence: the freedom to tell the truth and the courage to build something better.

I am running for Governor because I believe California can thrive again if we embrace Independence, balance, and an abundance ethos. My call to action is simple: join me in this independent vision. Join me in building a California rooted in logic, innovation, and respect. Together, we can prove that the government can deliver results when it answers only to the people.

Let's make California truly independent—purple in spirit, balanced in governance—and in doing so, create a future that works for everyone.

I dedicate this book to the women in my life—my mother, my sisters, my incredibly supportive wife, and especially my daughter, who has the longest future ahead. My deepest hope is to leave her, and her generation, a California worth inheriting.

—JON HENDERSON

PILLAR I

GROW

A FUTURE-FOCUSED ECONOMY

CHAPTER 1

ENDING HOMELESSNESS AND WILDFIRES THROUGH MASS TIMBER

BURN LESS, BUILD MORE

I am opening this book with these topics for one simple reason: I believe homelessness and wildfires are the two most urgent crises facing California, and I am prepared to hang my entire run for Governor on solving them. If we can fix housing and fire, we can restore safety, dignity, and opportunity for millions of Californians. Everything else flows from getting these two right.

Here's why Independence matters: entrenched interests on both sides have blocked practical fixes for years. As someone who left the safety of a big bank to build my own firm, I know firsthand the power of Independence. I didn't have to answer to bosses, shareholders, or corporate agendas—just my clients. That freedom to think and act independently is exactly what

California needs to finally address these crises without bending to partisan gridlock or special-interest lobbying.

I want to be clear: each chapter in this book connects with the others as part of a master plan for California. These are not one-off ideas thrown at the wall—they are interlocking solutions. In this case, a simple technology that already exists, mass timber, can be implemented at a massive scale in California to flip our current logging industry on its head and make exponential progress on net new housing units compared to the anemic pace we've gotten used to in recent years.

The American West is burning. Again.

For decades, we've watched billion-dollar fire suppression budgets fail to keep up. Meanwhile, the forests themselves are choked with undergrowth and overcrowded with small, fire-prone trees—exactly the type of fuel nature regularly clears out through low-intensity fires.

But we stopped letting those fires burn. We built homes too close to wildlands. We tied the hands of land managers. And now we're living with the consequences. The first time my wife and I lined up at the store for N95 masks was not because of COVID-19 but years earlier, when the first waves of raging wildfires in the Bay Area blanketed our skies with ominous, toxic smoke. That was when it hit me: wildfire was no longer a seasonal nuisance—it was a public health crisis.

What's gone wrong? Partisan stalemates and special interests block progress. Decades of poor forest policy, overzealous fire suppression, and lawsuits that prevent active management have created a massive buildup of fire fuel. Combine that with rising temperatures, drought conditions, and rapid exurban development—and we've created the perfect recipe for destructive megafires.

Every summer, firefighters risk their lives battling blazes that have no business growing so large. Insurance companies pull out of entire zip codes. Families lose homes. Air quality plummets. And yet the cycle repeats—because we're not addressing the root causes.

This one hits close to home. My brother-in-law, who married my oldest sister, retired after a multi-decade career as a battalion chief with the Ventura County Fire Department, and he is a wealth of information on this topic. But just as I heard the phone ring when I was a kid and watched my father get called away to the Rodney King riots to put his life at risk, my niece and nephew had to endure that same fear year after year during their childhood as their father was called away to confront the fires that others relied upon him to extinguish.

One refrain I hear from my clients who lean right is that regulations have restricted the removal of dead trees, effectively turning them into kindling on the forest floor. While the truth is more nuanced, outdated rules have created tinderbox conditions. And here again is where Independence matters: the current system is paralyzed by lawsuits and political gamesmanship. I don't owe allegiance to either camp, which means I can actually clear the way for practical reforms. Preventing the state from burning down and keeping Californians from paying four times more for fire insurance, if they can get coverage at all, should be a priority that rises above partisan stalemates. These kinds of outdated regulations should be reviewed and changed immediately. Let's turn that kindling into socially owned low-cost and no-cost housing we can be proud of.

THE SOLUTION IS ALREADY HERE: MASS TIMBER, AN INDEPENDENT ANSWER

There is a way to reduce fire risk while building affordable, sustainable housing. It's called mass timber, and it might be one of the smartest solutions we're ignoring.

Mass timber uses engineered wood products like CLT (cross-laminated timber) made from small-diameter trees—the exact ones we need to remove from our forests for fire prevention. These trees aren't suitable for traditional construction, but they're perfect for engineered wood. This is a textbook example of moving away from scarcity politics and toward abundance. For decades, these small-growth trees were considered useless, but in reality, we have an abundance of them. That abundance can be the key to unlocking solutions to two of our most pressing problems—homelessness and wildfire risk—at the same time.

I found Vaagen Timbers online while researching this topic, and the company has built a model that California could replicate: local forest-thinning contracts tied to local timber processing and construction. It's a closed-loop system that's good for forests, good for rural economies, and good for cities in need of more housing. Their use of the HewSaw—an imported machine that turns small trees into usable lumber—flips the traditional logging industry on its head in the best way. That kind of innovation can and should be replicated at the state level. This is where leadership matters: an independent Governor has the freedom to push forward bold, disruptive solutions like this without getting slowed down by partisan or industry pushback.

Examples exist around the world, like Brock Commons Tallwood House, an eighteen-story hybrid mass timber building at the University of British Columbia that was constructed in under seventy days; Mjøstårnet, an eighteen-story all-wood tower in Brumunddal, Norway, which was once the tallest timber building in the world; and Stockholm Wood City, a timber-built neighborhood in Sweden, with 2,000 homes planned by 2027, which will make it the largest project of its kind.

BURNING LESS, BUILDING MORE

This is the spirit of Independence for California: taking the best ideas, cutting through the noise, and building what works. Mass timber isn't a partisan idea. It's a practical, independent solution that reduces wildfire risk, creates jobs, and delivers housing at speed and scale. And it's exactly the kind of solution California will get when Independence—not politics—leads from the top.

INFLATION/DEFLATION LENS

From an economic standpoint, mass timber can be deflationary in two critical ways. First, by reducing the cost of new housing units, it lowers upward pressure on rents and home prices. Second, by reducing fire risk and stabilizing insurance markets, it lowers premiums that have been spiraling out of control. Independence matters here too: lobbyists for the insurance and construction industries resist disruption, but an independent leader can prioritize public benefit over corporate profits.

CALIFORNIA PATH

- **Build with California Wood, in California:** Set up a few regional plants that turn our thinned forest trees into mass timber for schools, affordable housing, and public buildings. That means fewer wildfires, more local jobs, and cheaper, safer homes.

- **Cut the Red Tape:** Approve safe, repeatable mass timber designs so projects get permits within sixty days instead of after years of waiting. If it's already been built safely once, we shouldn't make builders reinvent the wheel.
- **Unlock Accessory Dwelling Units (ADUs):** Make it easier for backyard units (ADUs/in-law units) to become fully deeded condos that families can sell or finance. Every ADU would come with solar panels and battery storage, and the main home would get upgraded too. To save water, lawns would be swapped for desert-friendly landscaping. We should also make it possible for first-time homebuyers to secure a studio unit for $50,000 or less, with financing readily available. This will give people an entry point into the marketplace, where they can build credit, move up as they outgrow their starter home, and—most importantly—stay off the streets.
- **Reward Fire Safety:** Homeowners who clear defensible space, retrofit for ember resistance, or live near undergrounded power lines should pay lower insurance premiums and get mortgage breaks. Protecting their homes saves them money.
- **Fix the Grid:** Start burying power lines in the riskiest fire zones first. Where private utilities won't invest, let's explore public or cooperative ownership. Overhead lines that remain can be upgraded with smarter, safer equipment.
- **Put People to Work:** Train California Department of Forestry and Fire Protection (CAL FIRE) crews, conservation corps, and convict crews to begin getting this work done immediately—thinning forests, milling timber, and build-

ing modular housing. Convicted people could work toward reentering society by reducing their sentences through wildfire prevention and construction projects. This builds skills, reduces recidivism, and strengthens communities.

FINAL THOUGHTS

This chapter represents the Independence ethos in action: finding solutions that entrenched powers have overlooked, scaling them with urgency, and delivering results without partisan spin. California deserves a Governor who can cut through the noise and build quickly and with integrity. Mass timber proves that when Independence leads, abundance follows. That's how we can end the cycle of fires, deliver affordable housing, and restore respect for what the government can do when it works for the people.

CHAPTER 2

UNEMPLOYMENT OVERHAUL

DIGNITY, NOT DEPENDENCY

This would be one of the very first systems I'd overhaul, because unemployment is fundamentally broken in both its design and its message. The current system often issues checks to people simply for being unemployed, without offering them a way to engage or grow during that time. While it's meant to be a safety net, it too often becomes a slow erosion of dignity, purpose, and contribution.

Let me be clear: I'm not saying we shouldn't support people through tough times. But today's model says, "You don't have a job? Here's money. Wait." That's not just inefficient—it's insulting. It strips people of momentum, weakens skills, and traps them in a loop of inertia. As a lifelong taxpayer, I've watched billions of dollars go into a system that helps no one grow. The longer someone stays unemployed, the harder it becomes to re-enter the workforce. We're not helping—we're warehousing potential.

THE FIX: EMPLOYMENT HUBS, NOT UNEMPLOYMENT OFFICES

I call this vision California Works. The idea is simple: take what is now the Employment Development Department (EDD) and transform it into a forward-looking Employment Hub network that actually connects people to work.

As an employer and small business owner, I've also seen how broken the current EDD is from the other side. The state's reliance on outdated COBOL-based computer systems during the pandemic became a national embarrassment—there were delays, fraud, and endless backlogs. California's workforce deserves better than fifty-year-old software. An independent leader can insist on moving California Works to modern, user-friendly platforms, disregarding 1970s standards. The EDD's website and processes are cumbersome and outdated—nowhere near as easy to use as modern payroll platforms or private software. Californians deserve government systems that meet the same standard of service and satisfaction they already get as clients in the private sector.

Here's the bold shift: shut down unemployment offices and replace them with Employment Hubs, places where you don't just file paperwork—you get a job that day. Not always your dream job, but real work that builds confidence, adds value, and keeps you moving forward.

The government's role should be simple: connect people being paid to do nothing with communities where something desperately needs to be done—whether that is cleaning roads, cooking meals, repairing trails, planting trees, or assisting the elderly. Instead of issuing checks for idleness, we create jobs with purpose—on day one.

HOW EMPLOYMENT HUBS WOULD WORK

These hubs would function like a hybrid of a job placement agency, a service organization, and a coaching platform. Community members could request help with real needs—painting a fence, fixing a community garden, or supporting the elderly. Workers would be matched immediately.

Flagship examples could include street and sidewalk cleaning modeled after the Gonzo Box initiative (see Chapter 10); forestry and fire mitigation using timber for housing materials; vertical farms and kitchens producing fresh food for communities; or construction crews building affordable housing and public works. Workers with specialized skills would be funneled into more advanced jobs that could lead to long-term careers.

The point isn't to keep people in these roles forever—it's to restore structure, momentum, and dignity while they bridge to their next opportunity.

RESETTING THE SOCIAL CONTRACT

Instead of "You don't have a job, so here's a check," the response becomes "You don't have a job, so here's a list of jobs available today. Pick one. Earn your check." That's not punishment. That's dignity. That's accountability. And it's fair—to the taxpayer, to the worker, and to the community.

Let's bring back purpose. Let's end dependency. Let's replace it with contribution, confidence, and a path forward.

This is how we shift from scarcity to abundance: every hour worked creates value for communities, builds workers' skills, and restores pride to the social contract. And because this book is a master plan, this ties directly to the vision laid out in later chapters, including the Citizen Status Card in Chapter 23. Work performed through California Works would immediately begin accruing points on their participants' cards, turning effort into opportunity. Instead of standing on the corner asking for change, they would build credit toward housing, training, and mobility with every hour worked.

When I first moved to the Bay Area, I saw homelessness in the Tenderloin in a way I had never seen before. My initial reaction, like many people's, was to want to help—to give money to those on the street. But I quickly realized that I could not help everybody. That experience changed me into a different kind of liberal: one who still wants to help but not by handing out dollars that perpetuate the problem. The real solution is to address the root cause and build a system that provides a dignified path for people to care for themselves—something our current structures fail to do.

INFLATION/DEFLATION LENS

Paying for inactivity is inflationary. Long spells on the sidelines erode individuals' skills, extend their claims, and push costs into healthcare, policing, and social services—while local businesses eat the bill for litter, blight, and lower foot traffic. Administrative churn (appeals, overpayments, fraud investigations) adds overhead without adding value.

Employment Hubs are deflationary: same-day work reduces claim duration, restores earnings quickly, reduces repeat assistance, and channels labor into visible civic improvements that boost local commerce. As a money manager, I want fewer dollars burned on friction and more invested in skills, productivity, and pride.

CALIFORNIA PATH

- **Modern Systems, Not COBOL Relics:** Replace the outdated 1970s codebase with modern, user-friendly software that pays workers quickly, prevents fraud, and restores trust.
- **Same-Day Jobs, Same-Day Pay:** Convert unemployment offices into dispatch hubs with morning roll calls. Workers choose from available jobs—earning wages and dignity immediately.
- **Skills to Careers:** Create ladders of badges (Safety → Tools → Trade Basics → Apprenticeship Ready) in partnership with unions and community colleges so that every shift worked builds toward a career.
- **Civic Backlog Pipeline:** Preload work orders from the California Department of Transportation (Caltrans), CAL FIRE, California's Department of Resources Recycling and Recovery (CalRecycle), state parks, cities, and school districts—so critical tasks like trail repair, firebreak clearing, and meal prep are tackled at scale.
- **Wraparound Support with Accountability:** Provide childcare stipends, transit passes, and coaching—so people can show up and succeed—while tracking results through a public dashboard that rewards contribution and transparency.

FINAL THOUGHTS

Unemployment should never mean idleness. It should mean transition, retraining, and opportunity. When people contribute, even in small ways, they keep their dignity, sharpen their skills, and strengthen their communities. That's the balance we need—compassion paired with accountability.

CHAPTER 3

THE PEOPLE'S PORTFOLIO

INVESTING IN MAIN STREET

This chapter introduces a common-sense solution: a California-based, county-driven public venture fund that does exactly what private venture capitalists (VCs) do—but for the people. Just like Marcus Lemonis does in *The Profit*, we identify small businesses that have the right people, a fixable process, and a compelling product—but are being held back by access to capital or strategic guidance. Local leaders, particularly mayors and regional economic boards, would be empowered to allocate funding to these high-potential businesses in exchange for equity—not just bailouts or loans, but real ownership that benefits the taxpayers who funded it. That's what I call a return on citizenship.

For too long, the American financial system has privileged Wall Street over Main Street. The lion's share of gains flows to institutional investors, hedge funds, and private equity firms, while ordinary families struggle to keep up with rising costs and stagnant wages. Even in California—the world's fourth-largest economy—most people don't feel like they have a stake in the prosperity their labor, taxes, and creativity generate. The promise of shared wealth has been replaced with speculation, volatility, and exclusion.

California's strength has always been its people. World-class universities, immigrant entrepreneurs, and diverse industries, from agriculture to aerospace to clean tech, are the natural feeders for a People's Portfolio—a system that allows everyday Californians to share in the upside their talent and innovation already generate.

My independent vision offers another way. Just as we can rethink energy, housing, and governance, we can also rethink finance. A People's Portfolio would give Californians a direct stake in their state's growth by channeling public assets—housing, infrastructure, climate resilience, and innovation—while giving residents a fair share of the returns. And only an independent Governor, free from donor capture or partisan games, can create a portfolio that works for Main Street instead of Wall Street.

THE CIRRUS STORY

The inspiration for The People's Portfolio comes, in part, from a personal experience. I am a pilot, and the aircraft company I love most is Cirrus. Two American brothers created it, introducing the revolutionary idea of equipping a small plane with a parachute—an innovation that saved lives and changed aviation. But when Cirrus needed capital to expand, no American investors were interested in funding them. Instead, the company had to turn overseas, ultimately to a company owned by the People's Republic of China. Today, Cirrus is no longer an American-owned firm.

That loss matters. It means American ingenuity was financed and captured by foreign capital because we lacked mechanisms to invest in our own innovators. If a company with a great product, solid processes, and committed people can't find American backing, something is broken. California should never be in the position of watching promising companies slip away because we didn't step up. The People's Portfolio is designed to change that. And Cirrus isn't alone—we've seen California-grown companies leave the state for lack of early support, only to flourish elsewhere. That is a missed opportunity we can prevent. Independence in leadership ensures that innovators aren't overlooked simply because they lack the right lobbyist or party ties. Entrenched interests and donor-driven politics have passed Cirrus by, but as an independent leader, I see the importance of backing innovators early, before they are lost to foreign ownership or forced to leave the state.

WHY A PEOPLE'S PORTFOLIO MATTERS

Partisan politics has left both workers and small businesses without support. My Independence allows me to design a system that works for Main Street, not Wall Street.

The concept is simple: if corporations and private equity funds can pool capital to generate outsized returns, why can't the people of California? Today, much of our state's wealth is siphoned off by external investors who profit from our real estate, utilities, and innovation ecosystems. The People's Portfolio would reverse that dynamic, keeping value here at home.

An independent approach ensures that investments are made on merit, not political favor. The People's Portfolio would operate free of donor influence and special-interest capture, giving Californians a direct stake in the prosperity they already help to create.

Key features might include a state-backed investment fund that takes stakes in strategic projects—renewable energy, affordable housing, transportation, and innovative companies—using a portion of state reserves and bond proceeds; citizen dividends, with a portion of the returns flowing back to residents, similar to Alaska's Permanent Fund but grounded in twenty-first-century industries rather than oil; and local reinvestment vehicles that allow counties and cities to pool capital for infrastructure, with state co-investment and guarantees.

This approach not only builds assets that Californians can see and use; it also creates long-term revenue streams that reduce the state's dependence on volatile income taxes from the wealthy few.

Funding for The People's Portfolio would not come from raising new taxes. Instead, the portfolio would be seeded with revenues from other programs described in this book that can generate surpluses. For example, excess solar energy produced during peak hours—once California owns its grid—could generate cash flow that gets recycled into the portfolio. A state Bitcoin reserve could also contribute, funded in part by cryptocurrency seized or recovered in criminal cases, as already happens in some states. Finally, profitability generated by prison reform and inmate labor programs—from bread baked to housing materials produced—could be reinvested in the penal system while also contributing to The People's Portfolio. Every inflow would be documented transparently, creating an investment-style ledger that treats all Californians as the portfolio's rightful shareholders.

THE FIDUCIARY PRINCIPLE AT SCALE

In my own financial practice, I've always believed in acting as a fiduciary—putting the client's interests ahead of my own. The People's Portfolio extends that principle to the government itself. The people are the clients. The state's duty is to grow its wealth, protect its capital, and ensure it has a real stake in the future.

Too often, financial innovation has been used to extract value rather than create it. A People's Portfolio flips that script by using professional investment management for the public good. This isn't charity. It's disciplined, returns-focused investing—directed toward projects that yield broad prosperity rather than narrow enrichment.

LEARNING FROM THE PAST, BUILDING FOR THE FUTURE

California has flirted with public wealth building before. The state retirement system (CalPERS) is one of the largest institutional investors in the world, but its benefits accrue to a specific group—public employees. The People's Portfolio would broaden that model, giving every Californian a piece of the action. Think of it as a mutual fund for the state, where the growth of California's economy directly strengthens the financial security of its people.

Other models exist abroad. Norway's sovereign wealth fund, seeded with oil revenues, is now one of the world's largest, providing stability and intergenerational wealth. Alaska's Permanent Fund distributes annual dividends to residents. But California doesn't need oil to build wealth. We have human capital, innovation, and the world's most dynamic industries. By channeling that into a People's Portfolio, we can create a renewable engine of shared prosperity.

VISIBLE WINS CALIFORNIANS CAN SEE

A People's Portfolio isn't just an idea for balance sheets—it's something families should feel. Imagine this:

A People's Portfolio isn't just an idea for balance sheets; it's something families should feel in their daily lives. Imagine dividend checks arriving in mailboxes each year, tied not to speculation but to the growth of California's real economy. Picture affordable housing developments financed through the fund, visibly improving communities as modular housing factories in the Central Valley produce thousands of units quickly and sustainably. Envision clean energy projects that reduce household bills while delivering long-term returns to the public. Think of innovative companies like Cirrus receiving the support they need to grow and stay in California, ensuring that their success benefits our residents rather than foreign investors.

These are not abstract benefits. They are tangible, visible wins—the kind of proof that the government can build. We could replicate the Lemonis model at the state level, creating synergy for all involved in giving our residents a share of the upside as local companies grow and thrive.

Scarcity politics tells us that wealth is limited and zero-sum. But California can demonstrate the opposite: that when people share ownership of the future, prosperity expands. A People's Portfolio would demonstrate what Independence looks like in financial form. It would be the government not just as regulator or redistributor but as builder and investor—acting independently on behalf of the people, not donors or parties.

INFLATION/DEFLATION LENS

The current financial model is inflationary in ways that matter most to Californians: capital flight drains value from our economy, leaving residents to shoulder rising costs while outside investors extract profits. A People's Portfolio is deflationary: it anchors wealth locally, generates stable dividends, reduces reliance on speculative markets, and funds projects that expand the supply of housing, energy, and infrastructure—thereby lowering costs while spreading prosperity.

CALIFORNIA PATH

- **Back Main Street Businesses:** Focus on companies with 10–250 employees that are profitable (or close to it) and just need help scaling up. Investments range from $250,000 to $5 million—enough to help a local manufacturer add a new line or a tech firm expand its payroll. Independence ensures that these decisions are based on merit, not political favors.
- **Keep Politics Out:** Elected officials can't touch the money. Investments are vetted by independent committees with strict conflict-of-interest rules because Independence is the safeguard against misuse.
- **Radical Transparency:** All investments, job numbers, wages, and tax receipts are published on the California blockchain, with a dashboard anyone can check. Independence means no hiding the ball.
- **Returns for the People:** Profits first refill the fund to sustain growth. After that, counties can either reduce local taxes or fees or send residents a modest annual dividend—a decision made by public vote, not political elites.
- **Rooted in California:** Guardrails ensure local companies grow and remain in-state, with a preference for employee ownership or in-state buyers to preserve prosperity.

FINAL THOUGHTS

This is about ownership—and Independence. California has the resources, innovation, and people to build a future where prosperity is broadly shared—not siphoned off by Wall Street, lobbyists, or partisan donors. Independence is the safeguard: it ensures that The People's Portfolio serves Californians themselves, not political donors, special interests, or outside investors. With a People's Portfolio, we can prove that Independence is not just a campaign theme but a system Californians can see, feel, and benefit from in their daily lives. And in doing so, California can once again show the nation that shared prosperity is not only possible—it's scalable.

CHAPTER 4

CANNABIS 2.0

A GREEN RUSH FOR THE GOLDEN STATE

America's relationship with cannabis is long and inconsistent. What was once demonized as a gateway drug has become a booming multibillion-dollar industry. Yet tens of thousands of Americans remain behind bars for the same actions companies now openly profit from. It's a moral contradiction that demands immediate reform.

For decades, we were told cannabis was dangerous—it was lumped in with heroin, PCP, and crack cocaine as a federal Schedule I drug. That classification marks cannabis as having "no medical use" and a "high potential for abuse." Both are provably false. Cannabis has been shown to help with pain, nausea, epilepsy, post-traumatic stress disorder, anxiety, and more. Meanwhile, destructive drugs like opioids, which have devastated entire communities through addiction and overdose, are classified differently and often prescribed by doctors. The hypocrisy is staggering.

In my experience, people don't break into their neighbor's

house to fund their next eighth of weed. It doesn't create a physical dependency cycle that leads to theft, violence, and collapsed families. Yet cannabis remains in the same legal bucket as substances that destroy lives. This was never about science—it was about politics, incarceration, and control.

ALCOHOL VERSUS CANNABIS: A CALIFORNIA DOUBLE STANDARD

In California, you can buy alcohol at nearly every grocery store, corner market, and gas station. Beer and wine flow freely at sporting events, concerts, and backyard barbecues. Two or three aisles in an average grocery store are devoted to alcohol—with brightly colored packaging that catches children's eyes decades before they'll be of age. Alcohol is everywhere, fueling entire industries and neighborhoods.

And let's be honest—alcohol is toxic. It contributes to DUIs, domestic violence, addiction, and long-term liver damage. It kills thousands every year. Cannabis, by contrast, has never caused a fatal overdose. Yet cannabis is still locked behind hyperregulation, plastic-sealed packaging, punitive taxes, and the lingering stigma of prohibition.

The irony is that while we treat alcohol as an accepted cultural staple, we've never allowed honest, large-scale testing of cannabis because of its Schedule I classification. That federal straitjacket has prevented decades of research that could have given us clearer data on its risks and benefits. Instead, we criminalized it, stigmatized it, and built an incarceration system around it.

Cannabis should be treated with the same social acceptance as alcohol, but with smarter regulation. If Californians can pick up a six-pack on a Sunday afternoon, they should be able to just as easily and responsibly buy cannabis flower or edibles at a local licensed shop without being priced into the black market.

A PERSONAL NOTE ON CANNABIS USE

I am a fan of cannabis and believe strongly in its many benefits, but I also recognize that I am not wired like most people. Everyone is different. Some people live their entire lives without using any substance, while others are naturally drawn to altering their state of mind to experience life through a different lens. I don't judge either path.

From my perspective, cannabis has many upsides. It grows naturally from the ground, requiring little more than soil, sun, and water. That alone tells me it is closer to California's natural abundance than many of the laboratory-manufactured substances people consume daily. For me, cannabis makes life lighter: comedies are funnier, food is tastier, colors are more vibrant. For those suffering from pain, anxiety, or stress, it can provide real relief without the destructive consequences of harder drugs or alcohol.

But cannabis isn't for everyone. For people who struggle with motivation, depression, or social isolation, it can narrow life instead of expanding it. I've never wrestled with depression, and I tend to wake up hungry for the day, with more passions than I have hours, so I find that cannabis complements a full life. For someone wired differently, it can become a reason to disengage and shrink their world. That is why I don't advocate cannabis for everyone—just for a society that treats it honestly, openly, and fairly so each adult can decide for themselves without stigma or fear.

Like everything else, balance matters. Cannabis use, like alcohol use, sugar intake, exercise, or work, requires moderation. Too much of anything can be harmful—even water in excess can kill. Cannabis demands nuance, and peeling back its layers is exactly the kind of work most people avoid but California needs.

COMMODITIZING CANNABIS

We should make cannabis a true commodity. Just as California homeowners should soon be able to sell kilowatt hours of solar power back to the grid at a transparent spot price, cannabis growers—large and small—should be able to sell pounds of cannabis into the system through licensed testing facilities, receiving the same public market price as any other grower. This kind of open, commodity-style marketplace would bring clarity, fairness, and stability. Every pound tested, tracked, and sold—just like oil, gold, or Bitcoin—would create a transparent market Californians can trust. It would also offer a path for our water-starved farmers in the Central Valley and Northern California. I see you, I hear you, and I want to work with you to modernize and increase your revenue tenfold through an abundance lens.

TOURISM AND REGIONAL GROWTH

Beyond cultivation, California can spark a boom in cannabis tourism. Each year Californians spend billions annually in Nevada—on vices marketed and celebrated at the state level in Las Vegas. We can bring that spending home by making the Emerald Triangle of Mendocino, Humboldt, and Trinity counties a destination on par with Napa or Vegas: a celebrated, legal hub for cannabis culture. With farm tours, lounges, festivals, and premium branding, we can turn today's hidden industry into a global draw for visitors, creating jobs and prosperity while addressing the environmental challenges those regions face, from landslides to wildfires. This is California's Green Rush for the Golden State.

INFLATION/DEFLATION LENS

Prohibition and overregulation are inflationary. We spend heavily on enforcement, courts, incarceration, cash-only operations, wasteful packaging, and a tax stack that props up the black market—keeping prices high and margins thin. A balanced regime is deflationary: lower, predictable taxes, simplified licensing, reusable packaging, safe banking, and bulk sales push out illicit suppliers, cut enforcement costs, stabilize prices, and expand legitimate payrolls. Just as California wine found its footing with sensible rules, cannabis deserves a framework that treats it like the agricultural product it is.

One of the most glaring examples of imbalance is taxation. At the federal level, because cannabis remains a Schedule I drug, businesses cannot deduct the cost of acquiring their product. That's insane. Imagine running a car dealership where you weren't allowed to deduct the cost of the cars you sell. You wouldn't be in business very long. Yet that is exactly the framework cannabis operators face today. It's punitive, irrational, and out of step with how other legal businesses are treated.

This distortion is inflationary by design—it forces businesses to raise prices to survive, which keeps the black market thriving. By contrast, a rational framework that lets cannabis businesses operate like every other enterprise would be profoundly deflationary. Instead of wasting money on redundant enforcement, unnecessary regulation, and punitive taxation, those dollars could be directed toward efficiency, lower consumer prices, safer workplaces, and public health initiatives.

CALIFORNIA PATH

- **Reset Taxes:** Keep cannabis affordable and competitive by capping total state and local taxes at no more than 15 percent. Replace confusing weight-based taxes with a clear, predictable system.
- **Simplify Licensing:** Create one simple state portal, with fair fees and quick approvals. Small growers and longtime operators shouldn't be buried in paperwork just to compete.
- **Reduce Waste:** Allow reusable containers with tamper-proof seals and encourage bulk sales to conserve resources, reduce plastic waste, and integrate the black market into one unified legal market—tested, tracked, and sold just like alcohol or energy.
- **Open Smoke Rooms:** Give adults over twenty-one a safe, licensed place to consume cannabis—much like bars or lounges for alcohol—while keeping front yards, schools, places of worship, and malls free from public smoking.
- **Grow Heritage Regions:** Build on California's new Cannabis Appellations of Origin (CAO) system. Protect heritage regions like the Emerald Triangle while establishing a system to recognize and safeguard strains, phenotypes, and genotypes. Mendocino, Humboldt, and Trinity counties can be positioned much like Napa Valley is for wine—as places of heritage and craft that attract tourists from around the world. With farm tours, tasting-style lounges, and premium branding, the Emerald Triangle could become a global destination for cannabis culture and tourism.

FINAL THOUGHTS

California has the chance to lead Cannabis 2.0 the right way—with fairness, balance, transparency, and abundance. By normalizing cannabis alongside alcohol but regulating it with more honesty and foresight, we can end the hypocrisy, boost our economy, and build an industry that works for everyone. The Golden State can make cannabis not just legal but safe and abundant and, in doing so, set the global gold standard for cannabis culture and commerce—leading the way for national reform.

California should not stop there. We must push for cannabis to be removed from its outdated Schedule I classification so that universities, especially our University of California (UC) system, can devote proper research to its full potential. That research could unlock tomorrow's anti-inflammatory and therapeutic treatments, positioning California at the forefront of medical innovation and cultural leadership.

CHAPTER 5

BITCOIN

DIGITAL GOLD FOR AN ABUNDANT FUTURE

UNDERSTANDING BITCOIN AND BLOCKCHAIN

As a fiduciary financial advisor, one of the major reasons I left a multinational bank after a successful twenty-year career was that I was not allowed to opine on Bitcoin's worthiness as an investment. That just wasn't good enough for me. This, combined with the fact that I was held to the suitability standard (a fundamentally lower bar than the fiduciary standard I'm now bound to as a Certified Financial Planner and Registered Investment Advisor), made clear to me that clients deserved better. They deserve a safe place to get informed, balanced information about all asset classes.

Whether those investments are right for them, clients should always be able to consult a knowledgeable advisor.

This was so important to me that I demonstrated my commitment by earning a certification in digital assets and blockchain—the Certificate in Blockchain and Digital Assets, or CBDA—created by the Digital Assets Council for Financial Professionals (DACFP), led by Ric Edelman. DACFP provides education and compliance, creating a designation rooted in traditional rules and transparency—standards sorely lacking in the shadowy corners of today's crypto landscape, where comprehensive, logical regulation isn't being implemented by the government.

I also want to be clear that I am not just a fiduciary and a new entrant to this market. I first discovered Bitcoin in 2017 when I opened my own Coinbase wallet and experienced the risks of self-custody firsthand. Since then, multiple clients have come into my office asking for help—some realizing in real time that their funds were gone after being tricked into transferring to fraudulent websites with look-alike URLs. These cases have primarily impacted younger male clients, in contrast to the elder fraud I more commonly see among older clients. The lack of clear regulation has created a breeding ground for theft and fraud. That is why I make a sharp distinction between the noise in the crypto market and what Bitcoin really represents.

So what is Bitcoin, really? It began with an eight-page white paper published in 2008 by someone (or some group) using the pseudonym Satoshi Nakamoto. That document was a blueprint for a peer-to-peer electronic cash system. Satoshi's true identity remains a mystery—some believe the author was a lone genius; others speculate it was a team of cryptographers. Other top picks include Hal Finney and Nick Szabo. Regardless of who it was, Bitcoin may well have been their gift to the world. I believe it was.

When I explain blockchain to clients and friends, I use two metaphors. First, think of a road. The road itself may be the same as it was decades ago, but the cars driving on it today are far more advanced—safer, faster, more efficient—than the obsolete cars of fifty years ago. Second, think of the internet. In the 1990s, early websites were clunky and basic. Today, websites and apps are polished, powerful, and integrated into every part of life. Blockchain is the new road, the new internet—the infrastructure layer. Crypto is the application layer that runs on top of it.

Right now, we're still in the junk-car and clunky-website era. Meme coins, scams, and illicit uses have clouded the conversation. But the future of blockchain will deliver applications that reduce the cost of trust and, in my opinion, help save our democracy. One of the most important of those is blockchain voting, which we'll discuss later in this book. Bitcoin, meanwhile, is the original application—a globally traded example of the basic plumbing that shows how a California blockchain could work.

I want California to build its own blockchain—an open, public system where any registered citizen can receive a wallet. That wallet could be used to participate in polls, provide input on public issues, and eventually even vote securely in elections. It would give us a real-time pulse of the public opinion, not filtered by the media or special interests. And it could do all of this cheaply, securely, and transparently. That is the future I believe California can and should lead toward. In this case, Bitcoin is the proof of concept, and California's blockchain is the next step.

When most people hear "Bitcoin," they think of headlines about price volatility, hype, or speculative trading. But as someone who has spent decades as a financial advisor, I see it differently: Bitcoin is not a casino—it's a store of value, a digital reserve asset, and a tool California should consider as part of a balanced and abundant financial future.

For centuries, societies have sought reliable stores of value.

Gold has played that role, providing stability across generations. But gold has limits: it is hard to transport, costly to secure, and difficult to divide. Bitcoin is often called "digital gold" because it offers many of the same protections—scarcity, durability, Independence from government control—while being far more portable and programmable. With only twenty-one million bitcoins ever to be created, its scarcity is hard-coded.

California, now the fourth-largest economy in the world, has long been the birthplace of innovation. From semiconductors to the internet, from biotech to clean energy, this state has led technological revolutions. Bitcoin and blockchain are no different. If California embraces them responsibly, we can lead the nation in transparency, financial resilience, and innovation.

A FIDUCIARY APPROACH TO A BITCOIN RESERVE

Prudence, not speculation, must guide policy. Maintaining a Bitcoin reserve for California would not be about taking reckless risks. It would be about diversification—just as any responsible family or institution diversifies a portfolio. Even a modest allocation—say 1–3 percent of reserves—could hedge against federal fiscal mismanagement and inflation, provide exposure to an emerging global reserve asset, and signal California's commitment to financial innovation. Unlike some other states that have used taxpayer dollars to build their reserves, California would not tap taxpayers for this. Instead, the reserve could be funded with proceeds from recovered assets from theft, fraud, and state-level prosecutions, turning wrongdoing into long-term resilience for the public good. Just as Norway's oil fund is publicly visible and widely respected, California could create a transparent Bitcoin Reserve Dashboard that shows taxpayers the holdings and their value in real time. Radical transparency is the antidote to skepticism. Done right, California could set the global standard for integrating digital assets into public finance.

BITCOIN VERSUS CRYPTO SPECULATION

It's important to draw a clear distinction between Bitcoin and the broader crypto industry. Many tokens are speculative, untested, or outright fraudulent. Bitcoin is different: it has survived for more than fifteen years, with a secure network and a predictable supply schedule. In fact, while there are tens of thousands of coins, Bitcoin and Ethereum together account for roughly 70 percent of the crypto market. That perspective shows how dominant the two truly are compared to the noise. California's role is not to chase every crypto trend but to recognize Bitcoin's unique role as a decentralized, censorship-resistant, and scarce asset. That focus protects Californians while signaling seriousness.

I entered the Bitcoin conversation not as a speculator but as a fiduciary. Clients asked me about it, and I needed to give them honest, informed advice. Over time, I came to see Bitcoin as more than an investment—it's an insurance policy against central bank overreach, inflation, and geopolitical instability. Just as I helped families diversify their retirement portfolios, I believe California should diversify its reserves. The same principles apply: don't overexpose, don't speculate, but don't ignore the opportunity either.

CALIFORNIA'S LEADERSHIP MOMENT

Imagine the signal California could send: the world's fourth-largest economy, known for technology and progress, responsibly incorporating Bitcoin into its reserves. Other states would follow. Nations would take note. And Californians themselves would see that their government is forward-looking, transparent, and committed to building financial resilience for future generations.

Beyond holding Bitcoin as a reserve, California can also lead in using blockchain to strengthen trust in the government. Voting systems, permitting, and financial disclosures could all benefit from blockchain's transparency. At the same time, consumer protection is critical. Too many people have been burned by unregulated exchanges or predatory schemes. California can create a regulatory framework that safeguards residents while welcoming legitimate innovation.

INFLATION/DEFLATION LENS

Ignoring innovation is inflationary. If California did so, it would spend more money chasing yesterday's tools while inflation eroded savings and fiscal uncertainty grew. A modest Bitcoin reserve is deflationary: it diversifies risk, protects purchasing power, and positions California as a safe haven for financial resilience. Just as mass timber turns wildfire risk into housing, Bitcoin can turn financial risk into resilience.

CALIFORNIA PATH

- **Build a Transparent Bitcoin Reserve:** Establish a modest, prudently scaled reserve funded by reclaimed assets, not taxpayers.
- **Protect Consumers and Investors:** Pair innovation with strong safeguards that distinguish Bitcoin from speculative assets.

- **Lead with Radical Transparency:** Launch a public Bitcoin Reserve Dashboard to show holdings and value in real time.
- **Educate and Innovate:** Empower universities and research centers to explore Bitcoin's energy, economic, and environmental impacts.
- **Power Governance Through Blockchain:** Develop a California blockchain platform for public input, permitting, and eventually secure digital voting.

FINAL THOUGHTS

California has always been a frontier of possibility. Embracing Bitcoin is not about hype—it's about prudence, transparency, and resilience. By treating Bitcoin as digital gold, we can diversify California's reserves, strengthen trust in government, and demonstrate abundance in action. The future belongs to those who prepare wisely, and California can once again lead the way—turning scarcity fears into resilience and opportunity. This is how independent thinking turns financial innovation into public resilience.

PILLAR II

BUILD

HOUSING, INFRASTRUCTURE, AND RESILIENCE

CHAPTER 6

HOUSING AT THE SPEED OF HENDERSON

FIXING CALIFORNIA'S HOUSING CRISIS

California's housing crisis is the defining challenge of our time. It is the root cause of so many other problems—homelessness, inequality, long commutes, and even our climate footprint. When homes are scarce and expensive, families are forced further from jobs, traffic worsens, emissions rise, and opportunity slips further out of reach. For too many Californians, the dream of homeownership has become impossible, and even renting feels precarious.

We know why: endless permitting delays, outdated zoning, and a regulatory environment that makes it faster to build a skyscraper in New York than a duplex in San Jose. What should take months takes years, and what should cost hundreds of thousands costs millions. California doesn't suffer from a lack of talent, capital, or demand—it suffers from a lack of speed and accountability.

THE SPEED OF HENDERSON

The phrase "Speed of Henderson" actually began as a criticism. When I launched Echo45 Advisors on February 21, 2020—the very day the stock market began falling due to COVID-19 fears—someone on the early team coined the phrase in a pejorative sense, meaning I had moved too quickly. Markets dropped by about 17 percent in the first week and roughly 37 percent in the first three months. But what seemed like terrible timing turned out to be a blessing. Clients were transferring their accounts during that downturn, and by the time the book had fully come over, markets had begun to recover and have largely climbed since.

The Speed of Henderson described how quickly I moved to implement new software, add services, update our website, or make decisions that required ripple effects across the firm. Not everyone likes working at that pace. But my current team thrives on it, and I've owned the phrase, transforming it into a positive. For me, the Speed of Henderson means that once I understand an issue, research it, and identify the best fix, I move quickly, efficiently, and cost-effectively to implement. It's not about rash decisions—it's about urgency, logic, and innovation.

The government must adopt that same mindset for housing. If Amazon can deliver a package overnight, why can't California deliver permits in ninety days? Bureaucratic bottlenecks don't just waste time—they destroy lives. Every year we delay another year, families pay inflated rents, young people postpone starting families, and workers and retirees flee to more affordable states. Independence from bureaucratic capture is essential—housing delivery must serve citizens, not processes.

REFORMING CEQA AND PERMITTING

The California Environmental Quality Act (CEQA) was passed with good intentions, but it has become a weapon for delay. Special interests exploit it to block projects, drive up costs, or simply take the NIMBY—not in my backyard—approach. NIMBYism has been especially strong in liberal enclaves like Berkeley or affluent neighborhoods of Los Angeles, where residents oppose replacing single-family homes with multi-unit housing. But a growing YIMBY (yes in my backyard) movement now recognizes that blocking housing supply ultimately hurts the very people progressives claim to help. I support the YIMBY approach and would make it logical, cost-effective, and proactive to add new housing units in California as quickly as possible. We need CEQA reform that maintains environmental protections while streamlining housing approvals. That means setting clear timelines, limiting frivolous lawsuits, and prioritizing housing near transit and jobs.

Permitting must also be radically simplified. Today, projects can be strangled by a maze of local reviews, each demanding tweaks and concessions until the economics no longer pencil out. We need a one-stop permitting process with strict deadlines—measured in weeks, not years—and overseen by independent fiduciaries responsible for measurable results.

UNLOCKING AFFORDABLE SUPPLY

California has tools to unlock supply without sacrificing quality. Accessory dwelling units (ADUs) empower homeowners to add small units quickly and affordably. Modular and prefabricated construction standardizes designs to slash costs and timelines. Mass timber is a safe, sustainable material that reduces emissions and accelerates construction. Public land partnerships bring underutilized state land into play for affordable housing projects.

These are not futuristic concepts. They are proven solutions waiting to be scaled. The difference is whether California has the political will to move with urgency.

I see this firsthand among many of my retired clients who are effectively house-poor. The only way they can unlock the equity in their home today is either by selling and downsizing—which often doesn't work in practice—or taking out a home equity line of credit. With interest rates higher in recent years, that option has not been attractive. A better path would be fast-tracking condo conversions. For example, someone with a one-acre lot could convert a quarter-acre condo and sell an ADU on that portion. In doing so, they would effectively sell a portion of their land value, while the buyer would gain affordable entry into the market. These ADUs could be required to meet criteria such as having solar panels, battery backup, no natural gas hookup, and low-water landscaping. This approach would both unlock equity for homeowners and expand the supply of affordable, sustainable housing.

MY OWN STORY

I know the power of opportunity because I've lived it. My first home was a condo at South Van Ness in San Francisco—a beautiful building developed by a man who is now one of my favorite clients. He is a deeply conservative man whom I respect greatly, and our relationship is built on mutual respect. We can talk about politics or anything else, learn from one another, and walk away without anger.

Years after I bought my first unit there, he explained that the first five homes in the building had been sold at an unusually low price. The sales company at the time was being compensated for speed, not for maximizing price. He quickly realized the mistake, replaced that firm, and adjusted course. I happened to be the fifth buyer, and what felt like a door opened by God set me on an entirely new path. I later bought another unit in the same building as a pied-à-terre when I was single, making good money, and working in Walnut Creek—always drawn back to the city I love so much.

That first break meant everything. I purchased my first home for approximately $315,000 and sold it two years later for about $555,000. Because it had been my primary residence for two of the last five years, I qualified for the $250,000 capital gains exclusion. That windfall allowed me to upsize to my next home, pay off student loans and credit card debt, and transition from being a have-not to a have. Step by step, that one opportunity set me on the path to financial Independence.

This experience reinforced for me one of the biggest truths in our society: whether you are a capitalist or not, everyone does better when society at large is healthier and happier. Housing opportunity shouldn't be a rare stroke of luck—it should be a foundation available to every Californian. Today, far too many Californians will never get that chance. That is not acceptable.

VISIBLE WINS

Housing reform must be measured not by legislation passed but by units built, and lives changed. Visible wins are key: families moving into affordable apartments, first-time buyers achieving homeownership, and young people remaining in California instead of moving away. We should set milestones and publish them so Californians can see progress. Government credibility depends on delivery—and leadership must act with fiduciary transparency to earn the trust of the people.

FROM SCARCITY TO ABUNDANCE

Scarcity politics suggests California doesn't have sufficient space. That is false. We have the land, the talent, and the capital. What we lack is urgency and Independence from political inertia. By cutting red tape, reforming CEQA, and unleashing modern building methods, we can build millions of homes, lower costs, and restore the California Dream.

INFLATION/DEFLATION LENS

Housing scarcity is inflationary. When supply is locked up, rents rise, commutes lengthen, and every dollar of income buys less security. Endless permitting churn adds costs without adding value. By contrast, abundant housing is deflationary. Faster approvals, modular methods, and smarter land use expand supply, stabilize rents, and reduce household costs. Abundance in housing lowers the pressure across the entire economy.

CALIFORNIA PATH

- **Protect Independence from Bureaucratic Capture:** Ensure the housing policy serves the people—not special interests—by empowering independent oversight and fiduciary accountability.
- **Declare Housing a Day One Priority:** Emphasize fiduciary stewardship—acting as a responsible steward of taxpayer dollars to deliver results efficiently and transparently. Commit to making housing the Governor's top mission

within the first one hundred days as an act of fiduciary duty to California's future.

- **Deliver Results Californians Can Trust:** Build or pave the way for 400,000 new homes in four years, and if granted a second term, aim for one million net new units, tracked transparently on a public housing dashboard.
- **Reform CEQA with Speed and Clarity:** Set firm timelines, limit frivolous lawsuits, and focus approvals near transit and jobs while insulating reforms from special-interest interference.
- **Guarantee Ninety-Day Digital Permitting:** Cut years of delay to months with one-stop, transparent approvals that restore confidence in government efficiency.
- **Unlock Land and Unleash Innovation:** Free California's housing policy from entrenched interests and political inertia, empowering independent action and innovation. Free up state and local land, scale ADUs and modular construction statewide, and empower independent builders to lead with speed and integrity.

FINAL THOUGHTS

Housing is not just about abundance—it's about Independence and fiduciary integrity, restoring trust through responsible stewardship and transparent leadership.

At the Speed of Henderson, we can deliver housing abundance rooted in Independence, accountability, and fiduciary ethics. Families deserve homes they can afford, workers deserve communities they can live in, and young people deserve the chance to build their futures here. Housing is not just about abundance—it's about restoring trust through responsible stewardship and independent leadership. It's time we built

California's future with urgency, balance, and vision—turning today's scarcity into tomorrow's opportunity.

CHAPTER 7

POWER TO THE PEOPLE

ENDING WILDFIRES, OWNING OUR GRID

California's energy system is broken. For more than a century, utilities have controlled much of the state's grid under the publicly traded model. The results speak for themselves: wildfires sparked by neglected equipment, blackouts during heat waves, skyrocketing rates. Billions are paid out in legal settlements instead of investments in safety. The model has failed. Californians pay the highest electricity prices in the nation, and in return, they get some of the least reliable service. That is not abundance—it is scarcity by design.

This is not just an infrastructure failure—it's a failure of dependent systems. For decades, California's grid has been beholden to corporate incentives and political inertia. True energy reform will require independent leadership and free-thinking solutions grounded in fiduciary responsibility to the public, not shareholders.

WHY THE PUBLICLY TRADED UTILITY MODEL CAN'T CONTINUE

The problem is bigger than any single company. It is the publicly traded utility model itself. While I strongly believe in publicly traded stocks for nearly everything else, I do not believe basic human needs—such as electricity, clean air, and clean water—should be compromised by shareholder interests. A utility's duty should be to provide safe, reliable, and affordable energy. Yet the incentives of a publicly traded utility push it toward profit extraction rather than service. The result has been more fires, more outages, more excuses, and more wealth extracted for shareholders while communities burn.

Californians deserve better. Electricity is not a luxury—it is the foundation of modern life. If the publicly traded model cannot provide safe, affordable, reliable power, then California must take responsibility for its own grid through independent, accountable governance.

PUBLIC OWNERSHIP AND LOCAL POWER

One path forward is public ownership. Municipal utilities, such as SMUD in Sacramento and the Los Angeles Department of Water and Power, consistently provide cheaper, safer, and cleaner power than investor-owned utilities. Why? Because they are accountable to the people they serve, not distant shareholders. Expanding this model across the state would align incentives with public safety and long-term investment.

But public ownership alone is not enough. We need to decentralize. Microgrids—local systems powered by renewables and backed by battery storage—can keep neighborhoods running even when the larger grid goes down. Schools, hospitals, and fire stations should never lose power during emergencies.

California has the technology and the talent to build a resilient distributed energy system. What we lack is independent leadership willing to move at the Speed of Henderson.

FROM FIRE RISK TO RESILIENCE

Decentralization itself is an act of Independence—local microgrids give communities the power to act without waiting for corporate or bureaucratic approval, restoring autonomy and security at the local level.

The same lines that carry power today are the lines that spark wildfires tomorrow. To protect Californians, we must bury or harden vulnerable transmission lines, aggressively deploy microgrids in high-risk communities, incentivize rooftop solar and storage for households and small businesses, and accelerate the transition to renewable generation paired with long-duration storage. By investing in resilience, we don't just reduce fire risk—we create jobs, cut emissions, and lower long-term costs.

California could be the world leader in rooftop solar, batteries, and fire-safe transmission. With same-day solar permits and installations completed in weeks rather than months, we could create real jobs and real pride—every neighborhood, every rooftop. We should go all in on undergrounding power lines. It costs more up front, but how many billions of dollars have we already spent rebuilding towns after wildfires? Every underground mile is a permanent insurance policy against the next Paradise or Palisades fire. If we flip the equation, California can not only meet its energy needs but also export clean power across the West. That means revenue. That means leverage. That means leadership rooted in Independence and accountability.

BUYING OUT THE GRID: THE NUMBERS

What would it cost to buy California's utilities at their current market capitalization? The numbers are big, but not unmanageable.

ELECTRIC UTILITIES

- Pacific Gas and Electric Company: $35.6 billion
- Edison International: $21.5 billion
- Sempra Energy: $47.0 billion (parent of SDG&E and SoCalGas)
- Algonquin Power & Utilities: $4.2 billion (owns Liberty Utilities)
- American States Water Company: $3.0 billion (owns Bear Valley Electric and water systems)
- Total electric buyout: $111.3 billion in market value as of October 2025

It's a big price tag—but compare it to the cost of rebuilding after wildfires, the healthcare toll from smoke, and the endless legal settlements. The money is already being spent—it's just flowing into the wrong hands. We could fund the buyout at market rate using green bonds, turning today's liability into tomorrow's asset—and restoring true Independence to California's energy future.

ENERGY ABUNDANCE AS A RIGHT

This principle is directly tied to California's independent vision—energy abundance must come from free-thinking leadership and local empowerment, ensuring that all Californians share in the prosperity of a transparent, people-first system.

Energy abundance means Californians should enjoy clean, affordable, reliable power without fear of blackout or fire. It means reimagining the grid as a public good, not a private monopoly. It means leading the nation in renewable deployment and storage innovation while ensuring equity—so that low-income families and renters, not just homeowners with rooftops, share in the benefits.

ELECTRIFY EVERYTHING

California can and should lead the nation in the Electrify Everything movement: converting homes, businesses, and transportation away from fossil fuels and into clean, renewable power. This means phasing out natural gas hookups in new buildings, incentivizing heat pumps and induction stoves, and ensuring that EV charging is as accessible as gasoline is today. It means streamlining permits so that when a water heater or furnace fails, the electric replacement is faster and cheaper than sticking with gas. It means making sure, through targeted rebates and subsidies, that renters and low-income families aren't left behind.

Electrification also aligns directly with California's broader vision for its future. Every electric car, bus, or train that runs on clean power reduces dependence on fossil fuels and cuts pollution. Our investment in high-speed rail and other mass transit will have a greater impact when powered by a resilient, renewable grid. This is the infrastructure of abundance: clean energy powering clean transportation, creating healthier communities and sustainable jobs.

A PERSONAL PERSPECTIVE

I drive a Rivian, and I love it. An American-made truck that is 100 percent electric with four independent motors—one at each wheel—it is faster, more capable, and more enjoyable to drive than any other car I've owned, and I have owned a lot of cars in my life. Powered by a plethora of solar panels in my backyard, which also serve as a massive shade structure for our painted deck, the Rivian represents my dream of a closed-loop of abundance.

My experience with solar power at my own home taught me firsthand how broken the current system is. We wanted to cover a large deck in the backyard, and installing solar panels gave us the chance to do so: create beautiful shade and generate renewable energy. Normally, people spend tens of thousands of dollars on umbrellas or shade structures. Instead, I built something that both improved my property and reduced my energy costs.

As a capitalist and a money manager for twenty-five years, I naturally look for ways to monetize assets—maybe even to a fault. What excited me most about solar energy was not only the potential to reduce my bill but also the possibility of selling power back to the grid. To me, kilowatt-hours are a commodity, just like barrels of oil or ounces of gold. Homeowners should be encouraged to generate as much power as possible, turning their rooftops into small energy businesses and creating a side hustle that generates meaningful income. I dreamt of powering my Rivian and our home and selling power back to the grid at a profit.

But the reality was maddening. The process took well over a year, with multiple rounds of reviews between the City of Walnut Creek and the utility. Each review chipped away at my original plan: fewer panels here, setbacks required there, extra wind-resistance standards layered on top. Ultimately, it felt like I was competing with the utility company itself. Rather than supporting my project, it seemed determined to make it so frustrating that I might quit. By the time my system was approved, it had been diluted and delayed by a year and a half—costing me thousands of dollars in lost opportunity.

CONFLICTS OF INTEREST AND TRUE WEALTH

I've spent twenty-five years working in the capital markets, and I believe deeply that is where true wealth is created. Investment, innovation, and entrepreneurship drive prosperity. But I also believe there is a fundamental conflict of interest when publicly traded companies control essential commodities like electricity. A utility company's first duty should be to provide safe, reliable, and affordable energy—not to maximize shareholder returns. Yet the incentives of a publicly traded utility push it toward profit extraction rather than service.

Energy is too essential to be treated as just another investment vehicle. We should provide it in the most logical, low-cost way possible. If California adopts rooftop solar, storage, and microgrids at scale, we could reach a point where, at certain times, electricity is essentially free. That is what abundance looks like.

Much like fast-tracking ADUs and allowing people to unlock equity in their homes without paying high interest rates, converting to a publicly owned and decentralized grid—where kilowatt-hours are bought at market rates, publicly posted, and always changing—would be another return on citizenship. This bold switch would directly benefit Californians. Doing the right thing would be incentivized with real dollars. Homeowners who invest in solar panels could realize direct financial returns by selling power back to the grid, transforming rooftops into long-term, income-generating assets.

Conflicts of interest should be eliminated wherever possible to ensure Californians receive the full benefit of available resources and innovations.

This is the same standard I hold myself to as a fiduciary. For twenty-five years, my work has been about putting clients first, removing conflicts of interest, and ensuring transparency. I believe the government should operate with the same ethic: act solely in the public interest, eliminate perverse incentives, and deliver results that build real wealth and security for Californians.

INFLATION/DEFLATION LENS

The current monopoly-driven energy model is inflationary. It drives up rates, concentrates wealth, and passes on the costs of failure—like wildfire settlements—to consumers. By contrast, decentralized renewables and microgrids are deflationary. They expand supply, reduce systemic risk, and stabilize prices. Every rooftop solar panel, every community battery, and every buried line lowers long-term costs while reducing disaster risk.

CALIFORNIA PATH

- **Reclaim the Grid for the People:** Transition publicly traded utility assets into public or cooperative ownership where feasible, using green bonds and fiduciary transparency.
- **Bury Fire-Prone Lines for Safety:** Prioritize undergrounding high-risk transmission corridors while upgrading the rest with smart, resilient technology.
- **Power Local Independence:** Install at least 1,000 new

microgrids in high-risk communities during the first term, ensuring critical infrastructure remains powered during crises.
- **Remove Conflicts of Interest, Empower Solar Expansion:** Eliminate the competition between homeowners and utility companies by aligning incentives—when Californians own the grid, every panel installed strengthens the system. More panels, sooner, benefits everyone.
- **Guarantee Fair Access for All:** Ensure renters and low-income families—not just homeowners—share benefits of solar and storage through equity-based incentives and community energy programs.

FINAL THOUGHTS

Energy abundance is not a dream—it is a necessity. Californians deserve power that is safe, reliable, and affordable. By breaking up monopolies, decentralizing supply, and investing in resilience, we can end the cycle of wildfires and blackouts, and safeguard our communities for generations. We can own our future grid, create local wealth, and prove that abundance is possible when we align incentives with people—not shareholders. California can show the world that clean energy abundance is not only possible but inevitable when we lead with vision, Independence, and fiduciary integrity.

CHAPTER 8

HIGH-SPEED RAIL AND BEYOND

BUILDING CALIFORNIA'S TRANSPORTATION FUTURE

California's high-speed rail project was supposed to be a symbol of progress. Voters approved it in 2008 based on its promise of connecting San Francisco to Los Angeles in under three hours. It was billed as a transformative project for the economy, the environment, and mobility. Yet more than fifteen years later, we have little to show for it besides spiraling costs, repeated delays, and growing public frustration. What should have been a triumph of vision has become a cautionary tale of dysfunction.

WHY HIGH-SPEED RAIL STILL MATTERS

Despite high-speed rail's failures so far, abandoning it would be a mistake. Done right, it remains essential for California's future. Transportation accounts for roughly 40 percent of the state's greenhouse gas emissions. High-speed rail could move millions of people quickly and cleanly, cutting car and air travel between regions. It could also unlock new housing corridors, enabling people to live in Central Valley cities while working in coastal hubs, relieving pressure on our most expensive housing markets. This is not just about trains—it's about reimagining how California will grow. High-speed rail would tie our state together, strengthen economic connections, and prove that we can still build big things.

California's failure wasn't in the idea—it was in the execution. Mismanagement, bloated procurement processes, endless environmental reviews, and political meddling turned a visionary project into a bureaucratic quagmire. Instead of focusing on the spine—San Francisco to Los Angeles—the project was segmented, undermining coherence and public trust. Costs ballooned, and the system was designed for delay, not delivery. We didn't build at the Speed of Henderson; we built at the speed of bureaucracy.

BUILDING AT THE SPEED OF HENDERSON

If Amazon can build warehouses in months and China can construct thousands of miles of high-speed rail in a decade, California should be able to finish one line between its two largest cities in less than half that time. What we need is discipline: reformed permitting, procurement accountability, and independent governance insulated from political interference. Most importantly, we must set clear milestones and deliver visible wins. Californians deserve to see trains running—first between Bakersfield and Merced, between Fresno and San Jose, and eventually along the full spine, from San Francisco to Los Angeles.

I've had the pleasure of visiting Europe several times, and on those trips I took the high-speed train between London and Paris. The ride was fast, enjoyable, and one of the most memorable parts of my travels. Watching the countryside fly past while I sipped coffee in a dining car was a reminder that transportation can be both efficient and delightful. Californians deserve that experience here at home. Imagine taking a high-speed train from San Francisco to Los Angeles with that same ease and enjoyment. Not only would we benefit, but people around the country would look to emulate us for our accomplishment.

BOOSTING TOURISM AND BUSINESS TRAVEL

High-speed rail would not just connect Californians—it would draw visitors from around the world. Tourists visiting the Golden Gate Bridge or Disneyland will have a seamless way to explore more of the state. Business travelers could move between Los Angeles, the Bay Area, and the Central Valley with speed and reliability, cutting wasted hours spent in airports and traffic. The economic lift from increased tourism, conventions, and business investment would be enormous, with benefits flowing to cities up and down the route.

High-speed rail would also reshape California's housing map. Reducing travel times between the Central Valley and coastal cities would make living in places like Fresno, Bakersfield, or Merced much more viable for people who work in Los Angeles or San Francisco. That shift could open new housing corridors, reduce pressure on our most expensive markets, and more evenly distribute opportunity across the state. Just as freeways defined California's growth in the twentieth century, high-speed rail could redefine it for the twenty-first.

Imagine boarding a train in Los Angeles and stepping off in San Francisco less than three hours later. No security lines, no traffic jams, no wasted hours. Along the way, cities like Fresno,

Bakersfield, and Merced are revitalized as hubs of commerce and affordable housing. Students attend colleges farther from home, workers commute across regions, and goods move more quickly and cleanly. High-speed rail could redefine what it means to live and work in California. This is abundance in action: faster connections, cleaner air, new housing opportunities, and a state that finally proves it can deliver the future it has promised.

INFLATION/DEFLATION LENS

Endless delays and rising costs are inflationary. They erode public trust and drive up the prices of labor, land, and materials every year. By contrast, visible wins and disciplined project delivery are deflationary. They stabilize expectations, reduce financing costs, and spread benefits quickly. Every mile built on time and on budget restores confidence and lowers long-term costs.

CALIFORNIA PATH

- **Recommit to the Core Vision:** Deliver the San Francisco–Los Angeles line as originally promised, connecting the state's two economic centers with urgency and discipline.
- **Empower Independent Delivery:** Establish an autonomous high-speed rail authority insulated from political interference, accountable only to results and fiduciary transparency.
- **Build at the Speed of Henderson:** Reform permitting and procurement with strict deadlines, performance-based contracts, and a public dashboard that shows progress.
- **Unlock Housing and Regional Opportunity:** Tie rail expansion to housing and job growth corridors in the Central Valley, creating affordable pathways to prosperity.

- **Deliver Visible Wins First:** Open the Bakersfield–Merced section within the first term to prove the model works and restore public trust.

FINAL THOUGHTS

California must finish what it started. High-speed rail is not just a project—it is a promise that we can still build boldly, still lead globally, and still deliver a future worthy of our people. If we have the courage to execute with Independence, fiduciary discipline, and speed, high-speed rail will be remembered not as California's failure but as the moment we proved that California can deliver abundance.

CHAPTER 9

CLIMATE, RESILIENCE, AND INSURANCE

PROTECTING CALIFORNIA'S FUTURE

Climate change is not a distant threat—it is here, reshaping Californians' lives daily. From wildfires that wipe out entire towns, to floods that devastate neighborhoods, to heat waves that strain our health systems and black out our power grid, climate risk is no longer theoretical. It is our new reality. And yet the systems designed to help people manage risk—particularly insurance—are crumbling just when Californians need them most.

THE INSURANCE RETREAT

Across the state, major insurers are pulling back. Homeowners in high-risk fire zones are seeing their policies canceled or their premiums skyrocket. Some families are being forced onto the state's bare-bones FAIR Plan, which offers minimal coverage at the highest cost. Businesses in flood-prone areas are struggling to secure affordable policies. The market is retreating precisely where it is needed most. Insurance is supposed to spread risk across a population so no single household bears the brunt of a disaster. But today, insurers are cherry-picking markets, leaving vulnerable communities exposed. This is not resilience—it is abandonment.

California can do better. We can establish a California Climate Insurance Program that pools risk statewide, ensures affordable coverage for homeowners and businesses, and ties premiums to investments in resilience. If your community fireproofs homes, clears defensible space, hardens infrastructure, or invests in flood control, your premiums should go down. Risk reduction should be rewarded, not ignored. Such a program could guarantee baseline coverage for every Californian, no matter where they live. It could use state-backed reinsurance to stabilize markets. And it could incentivize proactive investments in resilience, shifting the focus from disaster relief to disaster prevention. This is the fiduciary approach applied to climate risk: protecting people's assets while aligning incentives for smarter behavior.

Insurance alone is not the answer. It is a safety net, but the real work is reducing the risks themselves. California must fireproof communities by retrofitting homes, expanding defensible space programs, and undergrounding vulnerable power lines. We must upgrade flood protections in low-lying regions by investing in levees, wetlands, and natural buffers. And we must cool our cities with tree canopies, reflective surfaces, and climate-smart design to mitigate deadly heat waves. Every dollar spent on resilience saves many more in avoided losses. And unlike a payout after the fact, these investments improve lives every day.

As a financial planner, I have spent decades helping families manage risk. Insurance is a tool, but only if it works. Watching clients struggle to secure coverage for homes they have worked a lifetime to afford is infuriating. They've done everything right—saved, invested, bought a home—but find themselves unprotected when insurers decide the risk is too high. That is unacceptable in a state as wealthy and innovative as California. I have also experienced this personally. When my insurer abruptly withdrew Groveland, citing wildfire risks, my once-comprehensive policy was split in half. The FAIR Plan became my only option for fire coverage, while liability and other protections required a separate policy. The result? Nearly double the cost for far less coverage. That's not resilience—that's a system failure. My experience is not unique. As of 2025, nearly 600,000 California homes are covered by the FAIR Plan, which was designed as a backstop, not the main option. When the market abandons people at scale, the government must step in.

THE FIDUCIARY STANDARD FOR CLIMATE RISK

In finance, fiduciary duty requires putting the client's interests first, managing risk responsibly, and planning not just for today but for the decades ahead. That is exactly how California must treat climate risk. The people are the clients, and the government has a duty to protect their homes, livelihoods, and future. We cannot allow insurers or short-term politics to dictate outcomes. Instead, we must operate with transparency, long-term vision, and loyalty to those we serve. Climate resilience is not a discretionary expense—it is our fiduciary obligation.

Just as we've seen with electricity, the for-profit model for human needs is failing. Private utilities sparked wildfires. Private insurers fled high-risk areas. In both cases, profits were prioritized over public safety. California must explore socially owned insurance models—where profits aren't siphoned off but reinvested in resilience, prevention, and affordability. Instead of relying on insurers who leave when risks rise, we can build a system that adapts and protects. If we own the grid, as outlined in Chapter 7, and invest in mass timber and forest thinning, while putting people's needs ahead of shareholder profits, insurance costs will fall. When both ends of the spectrum—prevention and protection—are addressed with logic instead of blind faith in the free market, Californians will see lower premiums, safer communities, and a stronger economy.

INFLATION/DEFLATION LENS

Runaway suppression costs, premium spikes, and constant rebuilds are inflationary. They push insurance, construction, and municipal budgets higher year after year. Prevention is deflationary: systematic thinning, cultural burns, resilient infrastructure, and pooled insurance lower expected losses, stabilize premiums, and shorten recovery timelines. By shifting dollars from endless emergency response to up-front mitigation, we reduce volatility in both costs and lives.

CALIFORNIA PATH

- **Create a California Climate Insurance Program:** Guarantee baseline coverage and stabilize markets through statewide risk pooling and state-backed reinsurance.
- **Reward Prevention over Reaction:** Tie premiums directly to community resilience investments—rewarding defensible space, flood protection, and cooling infrastructure.
- **Fund Resilience the Fiduciary Way:** Use green bonds and

redirected settlement dollars to finance long-term resilience projects that lower costs for future generations.
- **Make Transparency the Standard:** Launch a public dashboard tracking premiums, claims, and resilience metrics so Californians can see results in real time.
- **Transition to Socially Owned Insurance Models:** Reinvest profits into prevention, affordability, and climate adaptation—ending the cycle of extraction and abandonment.

FINAL THOUGHTS

California must treat climate resilience and insurance reform as inseparable. Protecting homes means reducing risk up front and ensuring fair coverage after a natural disaster. Abundance means not accepting abandonment as the norm but building systems that protect every Californian. Done right, this chapter of our story won't be about disaster payouts—it will be about resilience, fairness, and shared security for generations. This is how we turn climate risk into resilience and transform scarcity into shared security.

CHAPTER 10

PRISON REFORM AND LABOR THAT HEALS

TURNING TIME SERVED INTO TIME INVESTED

California's prison system is broken. It warehouses tens of thousands of people at enormous taxpayer cost, cycling many of them back into society unprepared, unskilled, and still carrying the stigma of incarceration. The result is predictable: high recidivism, broken families, and communities trapped in cycles of poverty and crime. We spend billions reacting to failure instead of investing in success.

Today, prisons largely function as holding pens. Incarcerated people spend years behind bars with little access to meaningful work, education, or training. Taxpayers foot the bill for food, security, and basic healthcare, while getting almost nothing in return. Worse, once people are released, they often struggle to find jobs, housing, or support networks—making relapse into crime more likely. This is wasteful for the state and destructive for society.

The goal should be to keep people in jail for as little time as possible, reserving lengthy sentences only for the very worst offenders and uncontrollable, violent criminals. Nearly every other incarcerated person should have clear opportunities to actively work off their sentences through the reforms outlined in this book. True rehabilitation doesn't happen by sitting in a cell and being forced into racially segregated groups for protection and survival. It happens through meaningful work programs that contribute directly back to the community, supported by integrated therapy—both individual and group-based. What if time behind bars weren't just something to be endured—but something that could be earned back through service, growth, and real restitution?

I propose adopting the Delancey Street model across California's entire socially owned penal and rehabilitation system, eliminating for-profit prisons entirely. The Delancey Street approach blends intensive hard work with comprehensive individual and group therapy to eliminate idle time, increase productivity, instill discipline, and impart valuable skills. Upon successful completion, individuals are actively paired with employment opportunities, much like service members transitioning out of military service. If an individual fails, it indicates personal challenges rather than program deficiencies, given that so many others succeed. This model isn't a cure-all, but I believe it could address a significant share of the issues faced by California's incarcerated population, putting people to meaningful, productive work immediately if we have the political will to implement it.

The cost to house people in state-run facilities falls directly on the state, creating an incentive for effective rehabilitation rather than perpetual incarceration. Current incentives are skewed, with for-profit prisons financially motivated to maintain high prison populations without providing meaningful training or rehabilitation. My model flips these incentives. Properly implemented, a robust worker program can offset and even exceed the costs of incarceration, turning a burden into a benefit. Rather than aiming to keep people locked up indefinitely, the goal becomes to move them quickly through productive, supervised labor and into profitable employment. This shifts individuals from being a financial drain—receiving shelter, meals, and care that many working citizens struggle to secure—to becoming productive, self-sustaining contributors to their communities. Addressing this incentive imbalance is essential and urgent. We need to remove the conflict of interest, a core tenet of California 2.0.

I propose a structured model: each day of training or education completed counts as two days off, and each day of verified work counts as three days off. This labor must be meaningful, safe, compensated, and nonexploitative. It can be done in conjunction with local businesses—but never in direct competition with them. Instead of replacing external workers, incarcerated people would reduce their time in service, learn valuable skills, and be first in line for jobs if their post-release conduct and contributions prove worthy.

To make this real, partnerships are essential. Unions, community colleges, and private companies should be prepared to provide training, mentorship, and—critically—employment opportunities for those who successfully complete programs. If they benefit from an army of trained labor on the inside, they must also commit to hiring and supporting participants on the outside. This ensures the cycle does not continue in another incarceration but rather ends with a real career path.

Imagine a system where people reduce their sentences not just through good behavior but by learning marketable skills, earning certifications, and giving back to the communities they harmed. A young man convicted of car theft could study auto mechanics, welding, or electrical engineering and then apply those skills at state-run garages where residents receive free smog checks and low-cost maintenance—because it's in everyone's interest to keep safe, functional vehicles on the road. A woman convicted of drug distribution could earn a degree in addiction counseling and return to her community as a licensed recovery mentor. People convicted of vandalism could use their artistic talent to paint murals or contribute to neighborhood restoration.

The Delancey Street model operates businesses like restaurants and moving companies, employing rehabilitated workers, many of whom have been incarcerated. This model illustrates how structured purpose, skill-building, and accountability can translate into real-world success and set the tone for a broader network of restorative programs.

As structured rehabilitation transitions to civic contribution, several innovative models extend the Delancey approach beyond its original scope.

The Gonzo Box—named after our eighty-five-pound English bulldog—came from walking the streets of our "TenderNob" neighborhood in San Francisco and dealing firsthand with the sidewalk sanitation crisis. Gonzo Boxes would be near-indestructible kiosks stocked with cleaning tools—shovels, disinfectant, trash bags. Residents could sign up via an app to donate money or time, taking one- or two-hour shifts to clean their blocks. Two-person crews would service each zone 24/7, with trained incarcerated crews handling heavier biohazard cleanup, graffiti abatement, and repairs. The goal is dignity, cleanliness, and community ownership—neighbors taking pride and taking back their streets.

This same spirit of productivity extends to agriculture and food programs.

Vertical farming transforms rooftops and vacant land into productive agricultural spaces using recirculating hydroponics and stackable grow setups in repurposed shipping containers. Participants learn agricultural technology and urban farming and supply prisons, food banks, and community kitchens—reducing costs and improving nutrition. Where appropriate and legal, training could include cannabis cultivation on state-owned land, preparing graduates for legitimate work in a regulated industry. These farms—whether producing cannabis, lettuce, microgreens, or other crops—could operate around the clock, first feeding incarcerated populations and then selling surplus to local markets and restaurants. Every pound sold would generate income to sustain rehabilitation programs and provide healthy food at zero cost to taxpayers.

Building on that foundation, programs can move naturally into culinary, artistic, and construction initiatives.

Community Kitchens can train culinary crews using produce from vertical farms and on-site bakeries to provide nutritious, low-cost meals to underserved neighbors while teaching food safety, kitchen operations, and restaurant management. One signature program, **California Penal Code Sourdough**, would showcase bread baked by rehabilitation crews using locally milled flour. Each loaf sold in restaurants and cafés would fund a matching meal for unhoused or undernourished families, turning every purchase into an act of restoration. Like the broader Community Kitchens initiative, it would create a virtuous cycle of nourishment, dignity, and opportunity.

Dignity Works is a program that provides people with the opportunity to rebuild their lives and communities. Participants could join graffiti removal and public art crews that clean streets and transform walls into murals and sanctioned art spaces, restoring beauty and pride to neighborhoods. Others could work in fire prevention through partnerships in land management, reducing wildfire risk while earning certifications and valuable job skills. Construction training programs would turn fallen timber into affordable and transitional housing for Californians in need, while bakeries and mills would produce stone-ground flour and wholesome bread to feed prisons, shelters, and the public. At the heart of the program, each loaf of *California Penal Code Sourdough* would stand as a symbol of transformation—from punishment to nourishment, from stigma to pride, and from scarcity to abundance.

Solar installation training would prepare incarcerated workers to blanket government buildings, schools, and prisons with renewable energy. It's work that provides immediate impact and long-term savings, creating a cleaner, cooler, and more efficient California.

I believe in abundance: in turning scarcity into opportunity. Nowhere is that more urgent than in prison reform. I've spoken with clients and community members who believe strongly in accountability but also want to see redemption. As someone who works daily in fiduciary duty—aligning incentives and stewarding resources—I see incarceration as one of the greatest misalignments in our state. We spend staggering sums and receive very little return when we could be investing in people and communities instead.

I was reminded of this during our honeymoon in Singapore. It was shocking how different life felt in that city-state, which gets out in front of crime and homelessness—issues that simply don't exist there. Singapore is extremely safe despite its dense population. Gum isn't allowed into the country, and once you notice this, you can't unsee the difference: in the United States, gum is stuck everywhere—on streets, signs, and walls. We get used to living amid filth and neglect. A domestic version of this feeling comes when I walk through a Las Vegas casino or Disneyland, where private security, cameras, and constant upkeep create order and cleanliness. California deserves this same level of order and pride across our communities. If we achieve it, we won't just improve daily life—we'll also restore tourism dollars that our Golden State depends on.

INFLATION/DEFLATION LENS

Warehousing incarcerated people is inflationary. It consumes billions annually in stagnant costs—security, housing, healthcare—without producing value. Productive prison labor is deflationary. It reduces long-term costs by lowering recidivism, generates value through work that benefits the state, and creates future taxpayers instead of future prisoners. Every successful reintegration saves money and strengthens the economy.

California's prisons are distributed across the state, so rehabilitation efforts can be local and immediate. At any given time, roughly 89,000 people are in California state prisons. In several counties, the potential on-the-ground workforce is especially large: Kings County has about 12,000 inmates; Kern County nearly 12,000; Monterey County over 6,500; Solano County nearly 6,000; and Riverside County over 5,000. Add sizable centers in Madera, Sacramento, Tuolumne, San Diego, San Bernardino, and others, and you have a ready infrastructure for fire prevention, construction, and public works programs.

CALIFORNIA PATH

- **End For-Profit Prisons:** Replace profit motives with public accountability, ensuring that rehabilitation—not revenue—is the goal.
- **Labor That Heals:** Transform incarceration into productive, paid, and educational work that shortens sentences and restores dignity.
- **Public-Private Partnerships:** Link prisons with unions, community colleges, and local businesses to create job pipelines.
- **Measure What Matters:** Track recidivism, employment outcomes, and cost savings to prove success transparently.
- **Justice with a Fiduciary Duty:** Demand that California's justice system, like a financial fiduciary, operate in the best interest of the people.

FINAL THOUGHTS

California has a choice: keep pouring billions into a broken prison system or invest in a system of labor that heals. By turning time served into time invested, we can reduce crime, restore communities, and prove that abundance applies even here—in the places we've long written off as hopeless. True justice is not endless punishment. It is accountability, preparation, and the chance to come back stronger.

CHAPTER 11

IMMIGRATION AND LABOR

CALIFORNIA'S WORKFORCE FUTURE

For the past twenty-five years, I've worked with hundreds of families, and immigration is an issue that has always been at the forefront of people's minds. Throughout history and across societies, immigrants have been a convenient scapegoat for social problems when viewed through the populist lens of scarcity. I believe scarcity politics has led us to the brink of seeing one another—our friends and neighbors—as less than human. Things are boiling over, and people are becoming downright awful toward one another, especially online. Even in person, there's now a chilling effect: people hesitate to speak openly. Dog whistles—whether it's a hat, a shirt, the type of beer someone is drinking, or even a phrase—signal the echo chamber a person belongs to and whether you "speak the same language."

I believe most of us want the same basic things regarding immigration. After all, many of us can trace our family roots back just one or two generations. That diversity is our strength.

Much like a mutt that inherits the best traits from multiple lineages, America thrives because we combine the strengths of different backgrounds. Purebreds have their beauty but also their weaknesses. The same is true of monocultures in society. The beauty of our culture lies in strength when we invite others to join us—to help us get urgent work done and to build the California of tomorrow.

Through technology and common sense, I believe we can design a guest worker program that allows people to obtain valid identification, access many of the benefits of living and working in the US, and pay taxes on their earnings. With a relatively simple and navigable process, we can reduce the massive illegal immigration we see today and instead create a system that is both humane and efficient.

THE FEDERAL VERSUS STATE DIVIDE

Immigration is primarily a federal responsibility. The federal government controls who can enter, who gets visas, and who can naturalize. But California has wide latitude once people are here, from access to education and healthcare to labor rights, licensing, and integration programs. We can't issue our own green cards—but we can set the gold standard for how immigrants are treated and how their potential is unlocked.

Sanctuary cities in California have become targets of the federal government, and there is no reason to put a bigger target on our back than already exists. But compassion and decency must not be abandoned. We can defend our people without declaring open borders, and we can design systems that are humane, lawful, and transparent. As Ronald Reagan once said, "Virtually all of us as Americans trace our ancestry back to immigrants from distant lands, men and women who came to America with a firm willingness to work, asking only freedom." That truth should guide us now.

I don't believe it is fair to tell someone to pull themselves up by their bootstraps if they have no shoes. And it is not right to demand that immigrants come here legally when the legal pathways are so narrow as to be nearly impossible. I do not advocate for open borders. I advocate for clear, navigable hurdles—rules that any reasonable person can follow when seeking to work, study, and live peacefully in California. If they are willing to pay taxes, comply with the law, and help build our economy, then they should have a fair chance to join us in building abundance.

A PERSONAL PERSPECTIVE

I grew up in Southern California with many friends whose families had roots in Mexico. I have always loved Mexico's culture—the food, the zest for life, and the warmth of the people. My wife and I love it so much that, after being legally married at San Francisco City Hall, we chose to hold our wedding celebration in Cabo San Lucas. Ninety friends and family members joined us there, and the hospitality we experienced confirmed everything we already admired about the culture. I have traveled to Mexico many times and have never had any issues. That ease of passage stands in stark contrast to how complicated and inhospitable the US system often is for those trying to enter our country in good faith.

When we talk about building California's abundant future—whether the focus is making high-speed rail a reality, blanketing the state in solar panels, erecting wind turbines, or simply keeping our streets clean and public bathrooms maintained to an impeccable standard—we are going to need people willing to do hard work that many citizens I know wouldn't touch with a ten-foot pole. This is the kind of work that benefits every Californian but requires coordination, organization, and a mindful master plan. It will be implemented by those seeking to live in California and by those repaying their debt to society in our penal system. Both groups deserve pathways to contribute productively and to earn their place in building the future of this state.

STATE-LEVEL LEVERS CALIFORNIA CAN PULL

While the federal government continues to block many of the best and brightest from entering the country, California should lead by example and open its doors legally. We should establish a process to actively recruit top global talent to contribute to our already world-class UC system, propelling us into the next phase of invention and innovation. California should send a clear message that we believe in science and intend to lead the world in fields like AI, medicine, desalination technology, battery improvements, electrification, and other green technologies that don't compromise—much like Rivian embodies modern abundance. State-based programs can create immediate opportunities while setting examples for national reform. A California guest worker program could be fully documented and maintained on the California blockchain discussed throughout this book. This would be a prime example of how blockchain reduces the cost of trust in society, moving beyond cryptocurrencies to serve higher purposes like transparent labor systems, participatory governance, and eventually voting—helping restore our faith in democracy.

INFLATION/DEFLATION LENS

A shadow labor market is inherently inflationary. It drives down wages, fuels exploitation, and undermines legitimate businesses. Families pay hidden costs in depressed incomes, lost taxes, and community instability. By contrast, transparent, legal, and inclusive labor policy is profoundly deflationary. It stabilizes wages, boosts productivity, expands the tax base, and reduces enforcement costs. Bringing every worker into the open lowers costs, increases fairness, and gives California the workforce it needs to build abundance.

CALIFORNIA PATH

- **A Legal Pathway to Work:** Establish a state-based registry for essential industries and collaborate with Washington to pilot lawful, efficient worker programs.
- **Empower Dreamers and Talent:** Expand licensing, higher education, and professional opportunities for Dreamers and immigrant workers alike.
- **Protect Workers, Don't Exploit Them:** Enforce fair wages, workplace safety, and multilingual access to rights and resources.
- **Train and Integrate:** Partner with unions, colleges, and employers to create seamless pipelines from training to employment.
- **Modernize Through Technology:** Pioneer blockchain-based worker registries and portable benefits to ensure transparency and mobility.

FINAL THOUGHTS

California can build the most inclusive labor system in America. By turning undocumented work from the shadow economy into a transparent, productive system, we strengthen wages, boost fairness, and expand opportunity. Immigrant labor is not a liability—it is the foundation of abundance, and with smart reforms, California can lead the nation in proving it.

PILLAR III

GOVERN

MASTERY AND INTEGRITY

CHAPTER 12

TOUGH LOVE FOR VANDALISM AND SHOPLIFTING

POLICING WITH PURPOSE

Let's be real—this is the chapter where balance means making tough choices. It's where we admit that some of the criticism California hears from the right isn't just noise—it's frustration rooted in real failure. And as someone who has lived, worked, and loved deeply in the Bay Area, I can tell you that the shoplifting epidemic, especially in places like Oakland, is not just a talking point—it's a tragedy.

I've worked in Oakland twice—early in my career at Merrill Lynch and later, when I proudly returned home to the embattled city as a top producer. I built friendships there, celebrated the city's culture, and felt its grit and resilience. That's why it hurts to see what's happening now—crime eating away at a city I love.

Oakland has lost the Raiders, the A's, and more quietly, the confidence of businesses and residents. Among the worst culprits are petty theft and organized shoplifting, incidents of which are often blasted out on video like a feeding frenzy for pundits. But it's not just retail theft—it's the neighborhood-level crimes that leave people feeling like they're living in a dystopia.

A client told me her neighbor had a catalytic converter stolen—just a week after replacing the last one. This wasn't just the theft of a car part. It was a betrayal—stealing from someone you share a street with. That's what makes it so insidious: it is desperation turned toxic.

When I drive to the Oakland San Francisco Bay Airport and pull off on Hegenberger, I see the shuttered Walmart and In-N-Out—businesses that didn't fail but fled because of theft. That's not sustainable. And it's not something we should excuse.

So yes, I'm a bleeding-heart liberal when it comes to helping people who are struggling. But I'm also a die-hard conservative when it comes to protecting property rights. Those positions don't contradict each other. In fact, they reflect the same principle: treat others the way you'd want to be treated.

I recently discovered the work of Andrew Callaghan of Channel 5, and I've quickly become a huge fan of his reporting. His coverage of crime in downtown San Francisco—particularly in the Tenderloin, just blocks from where my wife and I lived in the TenderNob—showed just how far disorder had gone. In many cases, people weren't even locals; they were coming in from other cities to take advantage of the situation. That exposure made it clear to me: we can get ahead of this, but only if we have the political will to act.

I believe in balance: law enforcement respected but never above the law; communities safe but never silenced. We need courage that de-escalates, integrity that holds power accountable, and service that restores trust. The goal is a justice system that honors both liberty and safety—because real security comes from trust, not fear. My father was a police officer, and I grew up surrounded by men and women who wore the badge with honor. That experience gave me deep respect for the profession—and a clear-eyed view of where it needs to improve.

THE PROBLEM: OVERMILITARIZATION AND BROKEN TRUST

Too many officers are asked to be everything at once—therapists, crisis counselors, drug specialists, domestic violence responders, and occasionally peacekeepers. But they're given just a few months of training—far less than the years of preparation it takes to become a commercial pilot, an attorney, or a licensed tradesperson. We've upgraded the weapons, vehicles, and surveillance gear—but we haven't upgraded the training, standards, or conduct expectations. And the public knows it. Trust between law enforcement officers and the communities they serve has eroded, particularly in neighborhoods where the police presence feels more like surveillance than safety. The ripple effects of George Floyd's murder were not a blip—they were a reckoning. They revealed a broken culture and a system designed to protect itself, not evolve.

Let me be clear—I am very pro-cop. My father and many of the men I looked up to when I was growing up were sworn officers. I have deep respect for the profession and for those who do it with mastery. But I also remember the stories they told in hushed tones—about the abusers of authority who made their job harder, who crossed lines they knew shouldn't be crossed. And they were just as frustrated as the public was that the system rarely held those men accountable.

That's what this is about—accountability. Not fewer cops,

but better processes to weed out those unfit to wear the badge. And yes, more cops—especially walking beats, present in neighborhoods, not just in cruisers or behind barriers, and getting paid a better wage for the invaluable service they provide to the community.

A DIFFERENT APPROACH TO SAFETY

Dignity isn't about letting people get away with theft. It's about giving them a reason not to steal in the first place. And for those who still choose crime, the deterrent must be swift and overwhelming. Most people don't want to carry a gun—but they should feel empowered to call in fast, fearsome, and unmistakable protection.

As Governor, I'd flood our cities with peace officers—showing that California can handle its own safety solutions without waiting on federal intervention or outside mandates—not with semi-automatic rifles but with radios and training in psychology and de-escalation. There would be thousands of them across the state, and their job would be to observe, report, and route people into jobs and housing—and they'd call in the heavy team when needed. This is how we restore both safety and dignity. This is how we get out in front of the rampant squatting encampments, organized theft, and graffiti that have no place in the largest subnational economy on the planet.

As a private pilot, I know that safety can be achieved through process. I've seen firsthand how protocol, standardization, and accountability save lives. In aviation, mistakes are studied, not buried. When a plane goes down, we don't just blame the weather—we dig until we understand the system failure. Imagine if policing embraced the same safety culture as aviation—treating every use-of-force incident as pilots do near misses: debriefing it, analyzing what went wrong, and using those lessons to make the next encounter safer for everyone. Instead, we often see them doing the opposite: covering up internal issues, silencing whistleblowers, and transferring "problem cops" to new districts instead of removing them.

To make policing work, we must pair accountability with realism. Public safety reform also means addressing human behavior honestly. The Fix: Compassion with Consequences.

We build housing with mass timber and glulam technology—sustainable, scalable, fast. Staff those projects with inmates earning early release through skilled labor. Train people to build their future—literally.

Instead of warehousing people in jails, we make their time productive. Tie this to a modernized community policing model—where officers de-escalate first, observe and report proactively, and only escalate when absolutely necessary. This is law and order, delivered with empathy.

We also need to be clear about panhandling. Giving money on the corner doesn't solve homelessness—it enables it. Anyone who can sit for eight hours, asking for money, can do meaningful work, especially in a system where immediate jobs with same-day pay are available. That's dignity—not dependency.

When we met, my wife and I lived in the TenderNob—a gray zone between Nob Hill and the Tenderloin. We loved the diversity, the energy, the global mix of people. But the reality was brutal: stepping over bodies, dodging human waste, locking ourselves behind a garage "moat" at night. That experience transformed me into a different kind of liberal—one who wants to help but also wants to protect what we've built.

THE RED-LIGHT DISTRICT SOLUTION

Let's also be honest: humans have needs. If you don't provide toilets, people will use the street. If you don't regulate vice, it will spill into neighborhoods. That's why we need modern red-light districts—designated adults-only spaces in every major city where gambling, bars, and smoke rooms can be managed, taxed, and treated with safety in mind. Inside those zones, freedom is respected. Outside of them, penalties must be swift and serious. All of this, of course, would only be facilitated between consenting adults.

That's real balance: structured freedom, compassion with consequence, dignity for all.

My wife and I usually visit Las Vegas a few times a year, and we have clients there, so seeing them is one of the reasons we go. Whether friends want to meet us there, there is a convention we want to attend, or we just have free time and are looking for a party, Vegas is always open. It's the kind of place people head for bachelor or bachelorette parties, or maybe just a night out with the guys to place a few bets. But even in a space designed for fun, there's also a place for counseling and a way out.

I see these designated red-light districts as being similar to little Las Vegas's—self-contained zones for responsible recreation. Right now, Californians are leaving the state in huge numbers to experience exactly that in Nevada. Every year, we export an enormous amount of tourism spending across the border—money that could stay here at home, strengthen our economy, and help fund major public investments. To put it in perspective, even a single year of what Californians spend in Nevada could cover a significant share of the cost of transitioning our power system to citizen ownership, as outlined in Chapter 7.

So the question isn't whether people will spend the money—it's where. We can either keep exporting tens of billions of dollars to Nevada every year, or we can keep those revenues here at home, where they could help fund safe, responsible red-light districts, build community infrastructure, and even accelerate California's transition to citizen-owned energy. That's what abundance looks like: not moralizing about vice but channeling it into something that works for the people of this state.

INFLATION/DEFLATION LENS

Tolerating petty crime is inflationary. Store closures, retail "shrink" passed on as higher prices, rising insurance premiums, hardening costs (guards, bollards, cameras), and endless cleanup all strain city budgets and family wallets. Litigation and ER visits from preventable incidents increase costs.

A work-and-housing-first approach is deflationary: rapid shelter built with mass timber, same-day-pay civic jobs, restorative justice that repays victims, and targeted enforcement against organized fencing markets reduce repeat offenses, lower security and insurance costs, and sustain neighborhood commerce. The same principle applies to vice. Exporting tens of billions of dollars across state lines every year is inflationary—it drains our local economy and leaves taxpayers footing the bill. Well-regulated red-light districts would reverse that trend, keeping revenue in California and reinvesting in community safety, housing, and grid ownership, which ultimately lowers costs for families.

CALIFORNIA PATH

- **Dignity Works Corps and Gonzo Box:** Launch a statewide jobs program with same-day pay for graffiti removal, alley cleanup, block care, and 24/7 public bathrooms staffed by Gonzo Box attendants and inmate work crews.
- **Rapid Shelter and Transition Housing:** Deploy mass-timber micro-villages near transit with sobriety-neutral entry, 24/7 staffing, and a design that transitions people quickly to stability and Independence.
- **Retail Safety and Restorative Justice:** Concentrate unarmed peace officers in commercial zones, enforce swift restitution for theft, and route repeat offenders into Dignity Works rather than endless jail cycles.
- **Red-Light Zoning:** Authorize locally controlled adults-only zones with health services, sanitation, and security; outside-zone offenses face swift, certain penalties.
- **Speed of Henderson Deployments:** Commit to visible improvements within fifty days—clean streets, active patrols, functioning bathrooms, and transparent data—so Californians see change at the speed they deserve.

FINAL THOUGHTS

True Independence means Californians setting their own standards for safety, justice, and dignity—proving that the state can govern itself with accountability and trust.

Petty crime, shoplifting, and open-air despair aren't just statistics—they're signals of broken trust in our communities. California can't lead by excusing lawlessness. We must lead by proving that compassion and justice can coexist. Balance means structure, and structure means dignity. Order and dignity are the foundation of an abundant California. Policing with purpose means acting with fiduciary responsibility and urgency—delivering safety and dignity at the Speed of Henderson. When safety and dignity are restored, Californians will know that their government answers only to them.

CHAPTER 13

BLIND TRUSTS OR BUST

RESTORING TRUST IN GOVERNANCE

Public trust in government is at an all-time low. Scandals, conflicts of interest, and pay-to-play politics have created a system where voters assume their leaders are compromised before they even take office. In California—home to both immense wealth and immense need—the stakes couldn't be higher. When elected officials are influenced by private financial interests, every decision becomes suspect: zoning laws, contracts, tax breaks, environmental rules, energy projects, and beyond.

We cannot build an abundant future on a foundation of suspicion. Californians deserve leaders whose only interest is the public interest.

THE PROBLEM OF CONFLICTS

This isn't partisan—it's structural. It doesn't matter if a Democrat or a Republican is in office. We should never again have to ask whether someone is making decisions in their official capacity that could personally enrich them or their family. If we, the people, are going to grant leaders power over public funds, policy, and regulation, we cannot allow a conflict of interest to persist based solely on the hope that they'll be altruistic. That's naive. Many Americans already perceive Congress and statehouses as being full of self-dealing politicians. Whether that's true or not is irrelevant; we should make it impossible.

People need a reason to strive beyond money. Unfortunately, too many politicians have turned public office into an inside track to enrichment—a system where the fox too often runs the henhouse. That must stop.

BLIND TRUSTS: THE ONLY HONEST OPTION

The solution is simple: every elected official in California should be required to place their assets in a fully blind trust for the duration of their service. No exceptions. No loopholes. That means no stock picking, no private business deals, no self-dealing with real estate projects. Just a firewall of trust.

As Governor of California, I will place my own assets in a blind trust and have them managed by a third party for my family's benefit. That way, I can stop worrying about my money the way I do today and instead shift 100 percent of my focus to building a better California. This isn't just something I believe in theory—it's something I would personally practice. And I believe that every governor, state representative, and state senator, as well as every US representative and US senator, should be bound to the same policy. If that became law, I promise you we would see a dramatic shift in how lobbying and lawmaking work in this country.

Blind trusts aren't complicated. You hire a third-party manager to oversee your investments. You don't know what's in the portfolio. You don't get to make trading decisions. You don't tilt policy to benefit your holdings. And the public can rest assured that you're not double-dipping from both sides of the table. Professional, dispassionate money managers are everywhere. There's no excuse not to use them. The only reason not to adopt blind trusts is if you want to keep profiting off insider knowledge. What used to be a slimy practice among a select few now appears to be widespread among members of Congress. That has to stop.

FROM FIDUCIARY DUTY TO PUBLIC DUTY

As a fiduciary financial advisor, I am legally obligated to put my clients' interests ahead of my own. I can't buy a stock for a client because it benefits me. I can't steer them into investments that pay me hidden commissions. I act solely in their best interest—or I lose my license and my livelihood. Californians deserve that same level of fiduciary duty from their government.

When I say "fiduciary government," I mean that elected officials must be legally bound to act with loyalty and care for the people they serve, not their own portfolios. A blind trust is not punishment; it's freedom. Freedom from suspicion, from accusation, from the corrosive influence of private gain. It lets leaders focus on what matters: solving problems, not chasing profits.

INFLATION/DEFLATION LENS

Conflicted governance is inflationary. Every sweetheart deal, every tilted contract, every regulation bent for donors distorts the market and drives up costs for families. It creates hidden taxes in the form of higher utility bills, inflated housing costs, slower innovation, and wasted public funds. By contrast, blind trust governance is deflationary. It strips out the hidden costs of corruption, accelerates decision-making, and realigns incentives toward efficiency and fairness. When leaders act like fiduciaries, Californians get the government that works for them—not against them.

CALIFORNIA PATH

- **Mandatory Blind Trusts:** Require all elected officials and senior appointees to place assets in blind trusts before assuming office.
- **Ban on Stock Trading:** Prohibit lawmakers from buying or selling individual stocks while in office.
- **Public Fiduciary Standard:** Legally bind officials to a fiduciary duty to the people of California.
- **Real-Time Transparency:** Publish a clear, simple dashboard showing compliance with blind trust and anti-trading rules.
- **Enforcement with Teeth:** Create independent watchdog bodies empowered to audit, investigate, and sanction violators swiftly.

FINAL THOUGHTS

California can lead the nation by showing that democracy can be abundant—free from conflicts, grounded in fairness, and focused on outcomes. Blind trusts are not radical; they are common sense. If fiduciary duty is the standard for financial advisors like me, it should be the gold standard for the stewards of our state. Blind trusts or bust. And if you can't agree to that simple principle, then you shouldn't be in public service at all.

CHAPTER 14

VOTING ON THE BLOCKCHAIN

SECURING DEMOCRACY FOR THE DIGITAL AGE

Few things are more sacred in a democracy than the vote. And yet, in California and across the United States, our voting systems are outdated, expensive, and vulnerable to mistrust. Long lines, insecure machines, delayed counts, and partisan battles over access erode confidence in the very foundation of democracy.

California has the chance to lead with a bold solution: a blockchain-based voting system that is secure, transparent, efficient, and trustworthy.

VOTING AND THE COST OF TRUST

Gary Gensler, the former Securities and Exchange Commission (SEC) Chairman, is now widely disliked in the crypto community for having slowed the industry's growth—an ironic twist considering he once taught a course on blockchain at the Massachusetts Institute of Technology (MIT) and authored a white paper extolling its virtues. This duality between early advocate and tentative regulator underscores the tension between innovation and control at the heart of the crypto debate. In that MIT paper "Cryptocurrencies: Oversight of New Assets in the Digital Age," he wrote to the US House Committee on Agriculture on July 18, 2018:

> Though there are many technical and commercial challenges yet to overcome, blockchain technology has the potential to transform the world of finance by creating open protocols to which everyone has access, but nobody has control—to do for finance what the web did for information. The technology could reduce the "cost of trust"—the costs borne by transacting parties because they have to rely on their counterparties or a trusted intermediary to honestly record completion of the transaction.

That idea struck me as profound: blockchain reduces the cost of trust.

In our elections, the cost of trust is incredibly high. We spend billions on verifying ballots, fighting misinformation, litigating results, and securing physical and digital infrastructure. And still—half the country doesn't believe the outcome of major elections. That's not sustainable.

Blockchain could allow for a transparent, secure, and verifiable voting system. Voters could confirm that their vote was cast and counted—without ever revealing their identity. It could eliminate the need for third-party trust entirely. It would also render the concept of election "audits" virtually obsolete because everyone could see their own vote—live, recorded, immutable—in a decentralized ledger.

Think of this like a receipt you can't lose and that everyone can see, but only you know which one is yours. Imagine that voting involved the same transparency and traceability as viewing a public wallet on the blockchain—where only you know which wallet is yours, but anyone can verify that it exists and that a vote was registered to it. This preserves anonymity while ensuring integrity. Your identity stays private, but your vote's presence and accuracy remain publicly auditable. At any time, you can verify that your vote—for your chosen candidate or initiative—was recorded correctly. No ambiguity. No mystery. No room for "Stop the Steal" or conspiracy-laced recount dramas.

This is the kind of independent thinking California should champion: replacing scarcity-driven mistrust with a system that delivers confidence, transparency, and participation for everyone.

During every election, millions of Americans worry about fraud, suppression, or manipulation. Whether real or exaggerated, those fears corrode democracy. Without trust, participation drops and polarization grows.

Our current systems are expensive to administer and often inaccessible. Voting by mail is convenient but vulnerable to delays and disputes. In-person voting requires staffing, machines, and logistics that cost billions of dollars nationwide. And recounts drag on for weeks, leaving winners in limbo and fueling conspiracy theories.

Blockchain is not just about Bitcoin or crypto speculation—it's about trust. Just as the internet enabled instant communication and commerce, blockchain provides a secure, immutable ledger of transactions. Applied to voting, it could assign every registered voter a unique digital wallet tied to their verified identity. Each vote would be recorded as a permanent, transparent, tamper-proof transaction on the blockchain. Results could be audited instantly by anyone, eliminating the need for costly recounts. And most importantly, citizens could verify that their votes were counted without revealing how they voted.

This is the promise: a system where trust is built into the code, not left to partisan actors.

A CALIFORNIA BLOCKCHAIN

California can and should be the first state to deploy a public blockchain for civic purposes. Voting is the most obvious application, but the same infrastructure could support referendums, surveys, and even aspects of local governance. Imagine being able to instantly take the pulse of Californians on key issues—reliably, securely, and cheaply.

We discussed this earlier: reducing the cost of trust is one of the greatest opportunities of our time. Blockchain lets us do just that.

INFLATION/DEFLATION LENS

Our current voting system is inflationary. It consumes billions of dollars of equipment, staffing, lawsuits, and recounts—all to produce results that half the country doubts anyway. Blockchain voting would be deflationary: one secure infrastructure, reusable in every election, cutting costs while boosting confidence. Faster results, fewer disputes, lower costs. That's how you shrink the hidden tax of inefficiency.

CALIFORNIA PATH

- **Develop a California Blockchain:** Build a state-run, open-source blockchain tailored for secure voting and other civic functions.

- **Issue Digital Wallets to Voters:** Provide every registered Californian with a secure digital identity and wallet tied to the blockchain.
- **Pilot Local Elections First:** Test blockchain voting in city or county elections before scaling statewide.
- **Guarantee Transparency:** Make the code open-source and votes auditable in real time, while protecting privacy.
- **Integrate with Broader Governance:** Expand beyond elections to use the blockchain for surveys, initiatives, and participatory budgeting.

FINAL THOUGHTS

California has always led the nation in technology. It's time to apply that leadership to democracy itself. Blockchain voting could restore faith in elections, reduce costs, and empower citizens like never before. Trust is the currency of democracy—and with blockchain, we can make it abundant. This is how California can turn mistrust into resilience and scarcity into abundance in democracy.

CHAPTER 15

GUN POLICY IN A DIGITAL AGE

BALANCING RIGHTS AND RESPONSIBILITIES

The Second Amendment, ratified in 1791 as part of the Bill of Rights, says, "A well regulated Militia, being necessary to the security of a free State, the right of the people to keep and bear Arms shall not be infringed." That's the entirety of it—just twenty-seven words. That brevity and the open-ended nature of the language are exactly why there is so much contention around this amendment today.

I've spent much of my life around firearms. My father, a police officer for twenty-five years, had kept a loaded gun on the credenza in our living room since before I was born. Guns—respected, understood, and used responsibly—were part of our family culture. Today, I'm an avid competition shooter, passionate about the sport but frustrated by the regulatory complexities of owning and using firearms in California—a state many enthusiasts label as "behind enemy lines," "not a free state," or even "Communist."

As a responsible gun owner and a holder of an 03-FFL

(Curio & Relic) license, I've personally experienced the trade-offs involved in firearm regulation. One of the main reasons I obtained this license was to order ammunition directly to my home, a significant convenience in California. But that benefit came with accountability—I had to undergo a Live Scan fingerprinting process, effectively putting myself "on the grid." I'm also registered "on the grid" as a pilot with the FAA, a California-licensed tax preparer with the Internal Revenue Service, and an investment advisor with the SEC. I'm comfortable giving up some privacy for the privileges those licenses afford. When the stakes are high, I'll trade privacy for accountability. The same logic belongs in modern firearms policy.

The United States has more guns than people. While many are owned responsibly, far too many fall into the wrong hands. Mass shootings dominate headlines, while suicides by firearm remain tragically common, and illegal trafficking fuels violence in our cities. At the same time, many Californians—especially in rural areas—see firearms as essential for protection, sport, or tradition. These perspectives clash, fueling endless stalemates.

RIGHTS, RESPONSIBILITIES, AND LIMITS

Some argue that because the Second Amendment protects the right to bear arms, there should be no limits whatsoever. But no freedom works that way. Free speech, for example, is fundamental yet clearly limited: you can't shout "fire" in a crowded theater, spread libel or slander, or incite violence without consequences. Even in a democracy, rights evolve alongside technology and society to balance freedom with safety. The same must be true with guns. Unlimited access to any weapon—anywhere, anytime—is no more practical than unlimited speech.

This is where the balance of my upbringing comes into play.

I grew up around firearms, so they never carried the stigma for me that they do for many of my friends on the left. But I also grew up in California, with its dense population, where you simply can't have the same gun laws you might have on a ranch with one hundred acres of dangerous wildlife. And with a therapist for a mother, I came to understand both the need for guns and the need for balance. Guns themselves are not the cause of violent crimes—they are the symptom. To address the cause, especially in school shootings, we must focus on prevention: better role models for young men, more accessible mental health support, and proactive intervention when red flags or online manifestos emerge. Today, too much red tape prevents timely action. We need to flip that script.

California, however, has swung too far in the opposite direction. Laws mandating "featureless rifles" or banning pistol grips punish law-abiding citizens while doing nothing to stop criminals who can easily obtain weapons across our borders in Nevada, Arizona. The state's restrictive handgun roster makes it nearly impossible for new handguns to be approved for sale—a limitation many believe crosses into unconstitutional territory. We've also had "Freedom Week," when a federal judge allowed high-capacity magazines to be purchased legally in California for a brief period. For reasons that defy logic, those who bought them during that week can still legally use them, highlighting how inconsistent and ineffective the rules can be. These types of laws drive responsible gun owners out of state and cost California hundreds of millions—if not billions—of dollars in lost revenues from firearm manufacturers and related industries. Shooting sports—whether hunting, Steel Challenge, or United States Practical Shooting Association competitions—are part of California's culture too, and responsible citizens should not be pushed away.

Just as we regulate cars with licenses, registrations, and insurance, firearms should meet similar standards in the digital age. The principle is simple: rights come with responsibilities. Ownership should mean accountability—safe storage, verified training, and responsibility for how a weapon is used. And let me be clear—while I am strongly Pro-Second Amendment and believe deeply in supporting responsible gun ownership, I also believe in strict, uncompromising penalties for those who violate gun laws, especially when they use firearms in crimes against others. If you're using a gun unlawfully to harm someone, consequences should be severe and nonnegotiable.

DIGITAL TOOLS FOR GUN SAFETY

We live in a digital age where cars, phones, and even appliances are connected and traceable. Firearms, arguably more dangerous than any of these, remain stubbornly analog. That must change—but realistically, it won't happen overnight. Some smart-gun prototypes and biometric locks are being developed and gradually brought to market, but retrofitting the nation's existing stock of firearms is a long-term project. Those technologies are promising, but they are not yet a near-term solution.

The more practical near-term opportunity is blockchain. A blockchain-based registry could provide immutable, transparent, and low-cost records of ownership, transfers, and chain of custody. It would make straw purchases harder, theft easier to trace, and illegal trafficking more difficult. Privacy can be preserved by keeping personal data off-chain, with law enforcement access requiring judicial authorization. Ownership rights are preserved, while accountability becomes real.

PERSONAL RESPONSIBILITY AND CULTURE

At home, my firearms are secured and out of reach of unauthorized hands. Responsible ownership means making sure your tools of defense don't become tools of tragedy. My daughter is four and has never even seen my guns, but I look forward to the day when she is old enough for us to enjoy shooting together. Firearms should remain safely stored and inaccessible to minors or unauthorized persons, but on range day, few things compare to the rush of competition. That's why firearms remain integral to American identity, deeply enshrined in the Second Amendment—right after the First, which safeguards my ability to write this book openly.

INFLATION/DEFLATION LENS

Gun violence is inflationary. It drives up healthcare costs, law enforcement spending, insurance premiums, and the hidden tax of fear that erodes community life and local economies. A blockchain-based registry reduces illegal trafficking and makes stolen weapons easier to trace. Over time, as new technologies mature, safer storage and user-verification tools will further lower accidents and misuse. The near-term focus should be on systems that can be implemented quickly and at scale, to cut costs and save lives today.

CALIFORNIA PATH

- **Protect Second Amendment Freedoms Responsibly:** Uphold Californians' constitutional right to bear arms while ensuring balanced, accountable ownership through training and secure storage.
- **Modernize Firearms Oversight with Blockchain:** Use

technology to make ownership transparent, private, and traceable—creating a low-cost, immutable registry that stops crime without infringing rights.

- **Accountability Through Training and Licensing:** Establish verified education and licensing for all gun owners, just like driver's licenses, ensuring competence and accountability for every firearm.
- **Mental Health and Prevention First:** Invest in red flag awareness, mentorship, and counseling programs to prevent violence before it begins and address its root causes.
- **Lead as a Pro-Safety, Pro-Freedom State:** Prove that California can be both safe and free—leveraging innovation to protect rights, reduce fear, and rebuild trust between citizens and government.

FINAL THOUGHTS

California can lead the nation in moving beyond the stale gun debate by embracing technology and a balanced approach. Guns aren't going away—but gun violence doesn't have to be inevitable. By pairing rights with responsibilities, focusing on causes as well as symptoms, and matching analog weapons with digital tools, we can build a model of abundance: safer communities, lower costs, and a democracy rooted in both freedom and accountability. In that way, we honor the brevity of the Second Amendment's twenty-seven words while applying them wisely to a modern world.

PILLAR IV

INVENT

TECHNOLOGY FOR HUMAN PROGRESS

CHAPTER 16

WATER

CALIFORNIA'S LIFEBLOOD

California's relationship with water has always been fraught. From the aqueduct battles of the early twentieth century to today's debates about droughts, reservoirs, desalination, and conservation, water remains the state's most vital—and most contested—resource. Without water, California cannot thrive. Yet the way we currently manage it is outdated, fragmented, and often irrational.

THE PROBLEM: MORE PEOPLE, LESS ROOM FOR ERROR

California is estimated to need more than one million new housing units over the next decade, with nearly 180,000 needed immediately to relieve the pressure of our housing crisis. Those homes need water. Add in agriculture—which already consumes roughly 80 percent of the state's supply—and we're left with razor-thin margins. It's not that we don't have water. It's that we waste too much when it's plentiful, fail to capture enough when it's abundant, and allocate it poorly when it's scarce. If we don't act, water will become California's ultimate inflation driver—making food, housing, and insurance unaffordable while driving businesses and families out of the state.

THE ORANGE COUNTY MODEL: PROOF OF WHAT WORKS

Orange County's Groundwater Replenishment System is the largest advanced water purification project of its kind in the world. It takes highly treated wastewater and puts it through a three-step purification process—microfiltration, reverse osmosis, and ultraviolet light with hydrogen peroxide—to produce water that exceeds all state and federal drinking water standards. The system can produce up to 130 million gallons of drinking water daily, enough to meet the needs of nearly one million people. This model has been running successfully for more than a decade, proving that advanced recycling isn't theory—it's reality. The lesson for the rest of California is clear: replicate, scale, and tailor projects like this to local aquifers. The Bay Area, Central Valley, and Los Angeles Basin all have the opportunity to follow Orange County's lead, turning wastewater into a reliable supply while reducing dependence on imported water from fragile ecosystems like the Sacramento–San Joaquin Delta and the Colorado River.

THE FIX: BALANCE, TECHNOLOGY, AND COMMON SENSE

We must move from a scarcity mindset to an abundance model—one that uses technology, innovation, and common sense to unlock California's water potential. That means capturing and storing stormwater through underground cisterns, recharge basins, and floodplain restoration areas. It means replenishing aquifers modeled on Orange County's proven success and recycling wastewater to a potable standard—already cleaner than most tap water. Rebates should encourage desert landscaping and efficient irrigation instead of lawns, stretching every drop further. At the same time, we must invest in desalination powered by renewable energy, even if it's expensive now, because it is inevitable in the long term. Smart-grid water management, using Internet of Things sensors, blockchain-based rights tracking, and drone monitoring, can ensure efficient allocation. And allocation must be fair: California agriculture must continue to feed the world, but subsidies should reward efficiency, not waste. Wealthy enclaves should not enjoy lush golf courses while working-class communities face brown tap water.

DESALINATION: LESSONS FROM ISRAEL

Israel now gets roughly half of its water from desalination and other unconventional sources. Large-scale plants like Sorek provide a steady supply of potable water, helping the country withstand droughts that would cripple others. California can—and should—learn from this model. While desalination remains expensive and energy-intensive, it is becoming cheaper and cleaner with advances in renewable energy and technology. This is where the UC system and our innovation pipeline should shine. By leveraging research talent, H-1B visa recruits, and public-private partnerships, California could lead the world in reducing desalination and scaling it responsibly. And while many fear sea-level rise, desalination is one of the few direct ways to turn that challenge into an opportunity: hundreds of millions of gallons from the ocean to support life inland.

VERTICAL FARMING: MULTIPLYING OUTPUT, SAVING WATER

Eighty percent of California's water supply goes to agriculture, much of it used in water-intensive flood irrigation. But new methods like stackable vertical farming with recirculating hydroponic systems can produce five to ten times more output per acre while using only a fraction of the water. Crops like cannabis, butter lettuce, and microgreens can be grown indoors with precision, feeding both people and livestock. By working directly with farmers to adopt these technologies, California could slash water use, increase revenues, and stabilize food supply chains. This would be one of my top priorities in my first year in office: to prove that farming smarter—not just on a larger scale—can restore balance and prosperity.

DESERTSCAPING: BEAUTY WITHOUT WASTE

Lawns consume enormous amounts of water with little to show for it. California can dramatically reduce water usage by making desertscaping—low-flow, drought-tolerant, and zero-water landscaping—not only the norm but also the desirable aesthetic. Homeowners who want to unlock equity by adding ADUs through fast-tracked condo conversions should be required to implement desertscaping, paired with solar power, battery storage, and water-efficient systems. Master-planned communities should also aim for net-zero water usage through reuse and landscaping standards. Incentives could include tax credits or Citizen Status Card points (see Chapter 23) for households that make the switch. Every gallon not wasted on lawns can instead be redirected toward agriculture, food security, and safe drinking water for our children.

I've seen this problem firsthand as a financial advisor

working with farmers, builders, and families across the state. Water isn't just a commodity—it's the foundation of property values, food production, and quality of life. A shortage drives up costs across markets, from groceries to housing. And the uncertainty—never knowing if next year will bring drought or flood—creates volatility that punishes both businesses and families. We need predictability, not chaos.

INFLATION/DEFLATION LENS

Water mismanagement is inflationary. Every gallon wasted, every field left fallow, every crop lost to drought or flood drives up prices for families. Litigation over rights, endless environmental lawsuits, and political battles add overhead without creating any value. By contrast, investments in stormwater capture, recycling, desalination, vertical farming, and desertscaping are deflationary: they increase supply, stabilize prices, reduce uncertainty, and allow farmers and families to plan for the future.

CALIFORNIA PATH

- **Capture Stormwater:** Build large-scale infrastructure to store rain and runoff, especially in urban areas.
- **Recycle Wastewater:** Require advanced treatment facilities in every metro region to reuse sewage as safe, potable water.
- **Expand Desalination:** Invest in renewable-powered desalination plants, prioritizing drought-prone coastal regions and scaling innovation to drive costs down.
- **Restore Groundwater:** Actively recharge aquifers, rather than overdrawing, during wet years with excess water.
- **Smart Agriculture:** Partner with farmers to deploy preci-

sion irrigation, vertical farming, crop-switching incentives, soil-monitoring technology, and water-wise desertscaping.

FINAL THOUGHTS

California has the resources, technology, and ingenuity to solve its water crisis. What we lack is the political courage and coherent planning. By moving from scarcity thinking to an abundance strategy, we can turn water from a perennial crisis into a cornerstone of stability, growth, and resilience. Our future quite literally depends on it.

CHAPTER 17

ARTIFICIAL INTELLIGENCE

CALIFORNIA'S NEXT FRONTIER

I'll be honest. If not for artificial intelligence (AI), this book might never have been written. I've wanted to write for years, but sitting down to grind through thousands of words has always been tough for me. I have never done well with patience-heavy, linear tasks. Reading long books is a struggle. Writing one felt nearly impossible.

And yet here it is—an entire book written in just months, almost entirely late at night after I put our daughter to bed. That was possible because I had a writing partner who was always awake, always responsive, and never judgmental: artificial intelligence. I didn't outsource the writing—I still had to think, argue, and create—but AI gave me the same advantage a calculator gives someone who is bad at mental math. It leveled the playing field.

Few of us walk to work anymore because driving is faster and easier. None of us solves equations on an abacus because calculators exist. AI is the next leap forward. It's not about replacing human effort; it's about directing human effort where it actually matters.

Of course, that doesn't mean the fear isn't real. AI will displace workers. And the unsettling truth is that it threatens not only the low-skill jobs people have long worried about but also the professions that require years of schooling and memorization. If your career is built on absorbing and regurgitating information, AI will do it faster, cheaper, and likely better. This makes it unlike any tool before it—equally disruptive to the unskilled and the highly educated. That reality should unsettle us all. Or it can push us to think more creatively about how to harness it.

Artificial Intelligence is no longer science fiction. It is rapidly reshaping economies, industries, and daily life. For California—the global epicenter of technology—AI represents both a tremendous opportunity and a serious challenge. We must decide whether to lead responsibly or fall victim to forces beyond our control.

AI can be a powerful engine of productivity and innovation. From accelerating medical research to improving traffic flow to optimizing energy use to advancing education, the possibilities are staggering. At the same time, AI threatens to displace millions of jobs, concentrate wealth in the hands of a few, and amplify biases if not guided by clear principles. California, as home to Silicon Valley, Hollywood, and world-class universities, has both the responsibility and the capability to lead in setting those principles.

AI AND CALIFORNIA'S ECONOMY

California has more AI talent than almost anywhere in the world, but much of it is concentrated in a few companies. That concentration risks deepening inequality. We need policies that spread the benefits of AI more broadly—into agriculture, manufacturing, logistics, healthcare, and public services. Imagine AI helping farmers optimize water use or streamlining government paperwork so citizens spend less time in line and more time living their lives. As Governor, I would work with the visionary leaders of these companies to explore how their innovations can help solve some of California's greatest challenges—whether in water management, energy, housing, or transportation—using this rapidly emerging and transformative technology. That is the promise of applied AI in the public interest.

Automation has always threatened some jobs while creating others. But AI could accelerate displacement at a scale and pace we have not seen before. Customer service, driving, legal research, and even parts of medicine and finance are all vulnerable. People within the AI industry—those with far more knowledge than the average layperson—expect job displacement to occur faster and more extensively than most realize. California must be proactive in reskilling workers, building pathways from disappearing jobs to new ones, and ensuring that education and training systems keep pace with technological change. This ties directly into earlier chapters on prison reform, vertical farming, and renewable energy—areas where abundant new jobs can be created.

AI also reflects the data it is trained on, which means it can replicate and even magnify societal biases. Without careful oversight, algorithms can discriminate in hiring, lending, policing, and more. California should lead in setting transparency and accountability standards for AI systems—requiring explainability, auditing for bias, and ensuring redress when harm occurs. The goal is not to strangle innovation but to build trust and fairness into the systems that will shape our future.

SAN FRANCISCO'S ROLE IN AI

San Francisco was once the epicenter of the dot-com boom, and while it has struggled to find its rhythm since COVID-19, I believe another heyday is coming with the rise of AI. The irony of creation is that people need to come together face-to-face to build truly great things. Remote work offers efficiencies, but it can never fully replace in-person collaboration. With nearly all of the top AI companies already based in San Francisco, there is no reason they should not continue to grow, revitalize the Bay Area, and lead California into the next era of innovation. This revival must also connect to solving our housing and transportation challenges—because innovation requires places to live and ways to connect. As Governor, I would work directly with San Francisco's Mayor to ensure that these great companies—and the next generation of spin-off innovators—stay and grow in the city. We can once again make San Francisco the magnet for global talent it has always been, drawing the best and brightest from around the world who want to be part of the next great wave of California innovation, just as people did during the Gold Rush, the Summer of Love, and the dot-com boom.

As a financial advisor, I already see AI reshaping my own industry—automating research, generating financial plans, and even communicating with clients. Yet the human role—listening, empathizing, and guiding—remains irreplaceable. That balance is what I believe California must embrace: using AI to augment human potential, not replace it. If we get this right, California can model a society where technology empowers rather than dehumanizes.

AI AND ENERGY DEMAND

There's another reality we need to face: AI requires massive amounts of power. As more people and businesses adopt these tools in their daily lives, energy demand will surge. California must prepare now—by blanketing the state with solar panels, batteries, and other renewable energy sources—so that we not only meet this demand but also create a surplus. This connects directly with earlier chapters on energy Independence, grid ownership, and even water policy. Desalination and vertical farming both require vast energy inputs—AI-driven optimization paired with abundant clean power ensures we can tackle water scarcity, food security, and technological growth all at once. AI's future in California depends on abundant, reliable, and clean power.

INFLATION/DEFLATION LENS

AI has the potential to be profoundly deflationary—reducing costs in healthcare, energy, education, and government services. But unmanaged, it could be inflationary in another way: driving up inequality, fueling social unrest, and increasing the "hidden taxes" of instability. The balance depends on governance. California can show how to harness AI's deflationary power while protecting against its inflationary risks.

CALIFORNIA PATH

- **Lead with Transparency and Ethics:** Establish California as the national model for responsible AI development with enforceable standards for fairness, explainability, and bias prevention.
- **Reskill and Rebuild the Workforce:** Launch statewide

retraining programs that guide workers from vulnerable industries to high-value roles in technology, renewable energy, and infrastructure.
- **Empower AI for Public Good:** Deploy AI across state services—from transportation and healthcare to environmental management—to improve efficiency and citizen experience.
- **Invest in Clean Energy to Power AI:** Expand renewable infrastructure to ensure California has the energy Independence needed to sustainably fuel AI innovation.
- **Build the Next Generation of Talent:** Create an educational pipeline from high school through university that prepares students for an AI-driven economy and fosters innovation statewide.

FINAL THOUGHTS

AI will define the next chapter of California's story. We can either let it widen divides or shape it to serve everyone. By choosing transparency, fairness, and proactive adaptation, California can lead the world in demonstrating how AI creates Independence, resilience, and trust rather than fear.

CHAPTER 18

INNOVATION AND CLIMATE TECH

BUILDING CALIFORNIA'S NEXT ECONOMY

California has always been the world's test lab for innovation. From semiconductors to the internet, from clean energy to biotech, the breakthroughs of yesterday were born here. But in recent decades, we've ceded ground. Talent has fled to other states, startups have sold early to foreign investors, and regulations meant to protect the public have calcified into barriers that block deployment. If we want to lead the next century, California must recommit to being not just the place where ideas are born but the place where they are built, scaled, and independently owned by Californians.

THE MISSING LINK: DEPLOYMENT, NOT DISCOVERY

California is full of brilliant minds. Our universities, labs, and companies lead the world in new patents and research. But too often those breakthroughs get commercialized elsewhere. A desalination technology tested in San Diego might scale in

Israel. A solar breakthrough at Stanford might find its first customers in China. A battery technology pioneered in Berkeley might be manufactured in Nevada. The problem is not invention—it's deployment.

To change this, California must treat climate tech not just as science but as an industrial policy. That means aligning permitting, procurement, capital, and workforce systems to ensure that discoveries made here are built here—and that we maintain California-led ownership of the ideas, industries, and intellectual property that emerge from our state.

No state has a deeper bench of talent. We have coders in Silicon Valley, farmers in the Central Valley, aerospace engineers in Los Angeles, and climate scientists across the UC system. Pair that with urgency—wildfires, drought, and blackouts—and you have the conditions for breakthrough deployment. California has the need, the brains, and the market. What we lack is the political will to execute at the Speed of Henderson—our ethic of urgency paired with disciplined execution.

A FIDUCIARY APPROACH TO INNOVATION

Just as a fiduciary aligns investments with a client's goals, California must align its innovation ecosystem with the public's goals: affordability, resilience, and prosperity. That means directing state procurement toward California-made solutions, ensuring that local startups have customers from day one. It means streamlining permitting for climate tech facilities with guaranteed approval timelines. It also requires building public-private testbeds—such as microgrids, water recycling sites, and advanced manufacturing hubs—where innovators can prove and scale solutions on California soil. California must use its own capital, through green bonds, infrastructure banks, and pension funds, to anchor long-term climate tech investments. Finally, we need to train tomorrow's workforce through community colleges and apprenticeship programs directly tied to climate tech companies.

I grew up in a house where technology was always part of daily life. The first game console my dad brought home was Pong—an Atari model so early it didn't even take cartridges. From there, I owned every major gaming system that came along and eventually built my first gaming PC. That sparked a lifelong obsession with memory, processing speed, and keeping up with the bleeding edge. Upgrading a PC is a never-ending cycle: there's always a faster chip, a better card, a bigger drive. But that cycle taught me something important: if you want to stay competitive, you have to stay ahead of the curve. Waiting until you're too far behind costs more in the long run.

That's how I've run Echo45 Advisors, and it's how I would run California as Governor. Always invest in the best technology available because the returns on that investment multiply when applied at scale. That's how you avoid disasters like the COBOL code debacle at EDD or the Y2K panic—by modernizing early, not reacting late. The same principle applies to climate tech. The state should be a disciplined but bold early adopter so that Californians get the benefits first instead of watching others capitalize on our discoveries.

SPEAKING TO EVERYONE: FREE MARKETS AND PRACTICAL WINS

This isn't just about labs and left-leaning visions of climate policy. Farmers, contractors, and entrepreneurs know better than anyone that delayed action costs money. Rising water bills, blackouts that spoil crops, and wildfire smoke that cancels harvests are inflationary taxes paid by working families and small businesses. Deployment, on the other hand, is about lowering costs. Whether it's cheaper power from large-scale solar, reliable water from desalination, or faster permits that cut red tape, the message is the same: California must stay ahead of problems with practical, market-driven solutions. Free markets thrive when innovators can build and sell, not when they are strangled by outdated rules. This is about Independence through innovation—self-reliance, entrepreneurship, and letting Californians compete on a level playing field. Innovation here is not about ideology—it's about reducing costs, creating opportunity, and giving every Californian—from farmers to engineers—the tools to win.

THE POWER OF CREATION

There's another dimension to innovation that too often gets overlooked—the human bond that comes from creating together. Some of the strongest friendships of my life were forged through creativity: the bands I've played in, the songs I've written in tiny practice rooms, and the hours I've spent building something from nothing with people who started as strangers. Our wedding party was comically large because, by the time I married later in life, I had collected lifelong friends from these shared creative experiences. Whether it's playing music, building a car in a shop, serving alongside others in the military, or constructing something tangible and lasting, creation builds respect. Working toward a shared goal and notching real wins together changes how we see one another. It reminds us that shared accomplishment—especially through work that matters—creates unity, trust, and prosperity.

These same principles apply to innovation and climate technology. Working side by side to build California's next economy will not just strengthen our infrastructure—it will strengthen our communities. The act of creation itself fosters connection, respect, and pride. If we can channel that energy across our industries, from climate tech to construction to education, those notched wins will unlock a new wave of prosperity and shared purpose across the Golden State.

INFLATION/DEFLATION LENS

Scarcity politics tells us innovation is expensive. In reality, delayed deployment is inflationary—every year without desalination, water costs rise. For example, drought-driven reliance on imported water has raised urban water rates by double digits in some districts. Every year that we don't have local battery factories, grid storage prices stay high. By contrast, rapid deployment is deflationary: large-scale solar projects cut energy bills, local manufacturing lowers costs, and resilient infrastructure reduces the hidden taxes of disaster. Independent leadership ensures that California builds more quickly, more intelligently, and in the service of its own people. Abundance comes from building faster.

CALIFORNIA PATH

- **Deploy, Don't Delay:** Establish a California Climate Tech Deployment Authority to fast-track permitting, financing, and procurement so ideas turn into industries.
- **Buy California First:** Require state agencies to source a portion of contracts from in-state climate tech companies to create local demand and jobs.
- **Finance the Future:** Expand green bond programs and

leverage pension funds to build large-scale water, energy, and resilience projects.
- **Train for Tomorrow:** Launch a California Climate Corps and apprenticeships to train thousands of workers in the energy, water, and materials industries.
- **Build Statewide Hubs:** Create regional innovation centers across the Bay Area, Central Valley, Inland Empire, and San Diego so deployment reaches every corner of the state.

FINAL THOUGHTS

California's future depends on our ability to move from ideas to impact. Innovation without deployment is wasted potential. But if we align talent, capital, and political will, we can build the next economy—an economy rooted in Independence and abundance—right here. This is how California not only survives the climate crisis but leads the world out of it.

PILLAR V

DEPLOY

A SOCIAL CONTRACT THAT WORKS

CHAPTER 19

DMV 2.0

REINVENTING PUBLIC SERVICE IN CALIFORNIA

For most Californians, government isn't experienced through grand speeches or trillion-dollar budgets—it's experienced through the Department of Motor Vehicles (DMV). It's standing in line, pulling a ticket, and sitting for hours under fluorescent lights while waiting for your number to be called. It's the feeling of being stuck in detention for the crime of needing to register your car. And for the workers behind the counter, it's the grind of repeating the same frustrating interactions all day, bearing the weight of citizen anger. That's the daily interface between Californians and their state—and for too long, it has symbolized frustration rather than competence.

The truth is that people don't live in policy abstractions. They live in real time. And when hours of their lives are lost to outdated processes, that's the government failing them in the most personal way. DMV reform isn't glamorous, but it's where government credibility is either built or broken. If we fix this, we fix the very relationship Californians have with their state.

PERSONAL EXPERIENCE

Getting a notice that I have to report to the DMV feels a lot like being called for jury duty—it's not the task itself that I dread; it's the inefficiency. I hate inefficiencies. I hate working for people or within systems that are slower and less logical than I know they could be. With just a couple of simple improvements, so many lost hours and so much frustration could be avoided. This is one of the reasons I decided to run for Governor: for too long, I assumed that government leaders cared about efficiency the way I do, but the outcomes don't align. If we focus on what most directly affects daily life, we can save people not just money but time, patience, and emotional strain. Less money wasted. Fewer hours lost. Less energy drained. That's the real measure of good government. As a fiduciary, I believe Californians deserve a return not only on their tax dollars but also on their time. The government should treat every wasted hour as seriously as every wasted dollar—because both are assets that belong to the people.

CITIZEN FRUSTRATION

I hear it all the time from my clients: outrage at the cost of car registration, parking tickets, and other state-imposed fees. They feel like they're being taxed endlessly but don't see those dollars invested in anything they can be proud of. That perception is powerful—and it drives people away from California just as much as real costs do. The truth is that we can overcome this with simple enhancements to the way we deliver services. When people feel respected, efficient service turns frustration into pride, and confidence in the state begins to return. And when fees are paired with visible improvements, citizens begin to see them not as punishment but as investment—fulfilling the fiduciary duty their government owes them.

TOWARD A NEW MODEL OF SERVICE

The DMV should feel less like detention and more like an Apple Store—bright, efficient, welcoming, and intuitive. Citizens should walk away not only with their paperwork complete but with the feeling that their time was respected. Technology already exists to make this happen: online check-ins, real-time wait times, AI-driven form assistance, and digital IDs that reduce paperwork and in-person visits. These tools can transform the DMV from a bottleneck into a benchmark for public service.

This transformation isn't just about convenience. It's about dignity. When people leave a public institution feeling respected, they regain faith in their government. And when workers are equipped with modern systems instead of outdated bureaucracy, they take pride in their service instead of absorbing citizen frustration. DMV 2.0 can be the blueprint for modernizing every state-run institution—from libraries to licensing—placing citizens, rather than bureaucracy, at the center.

EXPANDING TO PUBLIC TRANSIT

The same logic that applies to DMV reform must apply to public transit. From Bay Area Rapid Transit (BART) and Muni in the Bay Area to LA Metro, San Diego's trolleys, Caltrain, the Coaster, and even the state's ferries, every mode of public transit should be modernized, enhanced, and optimized to reduce waste. This means better scheduling, streamlined ticketing, real-time tracking, and customer service that respects the rider. Just as importantly, we must transition all government vehicles—buses, trains, police cruisers, and maintenance fleets—toward electrification. The future of public service is clean, efficient, and citizen-centered. Artificial intelligence can help dramatically reduce waste—optimizing traffic lights so drivers spend less of their day stuck at empty intersections and improving bus and train schedules to prevent both overcrowding and empty runs. Smarter systems mean more reliable service, less wasted energy, and a better experience for everyone.

RETURN ON CITIZENSHIP

Throughout this book, I discuss a return on citizenship—whether it's community-owned energy grids or citizen-driven insurance pools. Here, the return is measured in time. People either have money or they have time, but rarely both. Time is the resource that most Californians can least afford to lose. DMV 2.0 and public service modernization give that time back. Every hour saved is a dividend of citizenship, restoring one of life's most precious assets to the people of California.

INFLATION/DEFLATION LENS

Lost hours are inflationary. Every extra minute in a DMV line is productivity gone—missed shifts, added childcare costs, lost opportunities. Outdated processes increase state costs through inefficiency, errors, and redundant labor. Citizens pay twice: once in taxes and again in lost time.

A streamlined DMV is deflationary. By moving services online, eliminating redundant steps, and reducing error rates, we save Californians millions of hours per year. That's a direct return of time—our most finite resource—back to the people. Efficiency lowers operating costs for the state and reduces the hidden "time tax" that every Californian currently pays.

CALIFORNIA PATH

- **Apple Store Model:** Redesign DMV offices as bright, intuitive, and service-centered spaces that respect citizens' time and dignity.
- **Digital-First and AI Optimization:** Expand online renewals, digital IDs, information on real-time wait times, and AI-assisted form completion—while also using AI to optimize traffic lights, bus routes, and train schedules to reduce waste and improve service.
- **Workforce Empowerment:** Equip employees with modern tools, better training, and performance incentives that reward efficiency and service quality.
- **Integrated Public Service and Transit Modernization:** Create one-stop platforms that combine DMV functions with other state services and modernize public transit systems—electrifying government fleets and improving rider experience statewide.
- **Speed of Henderson Standards:** Commit to measurable improvements within months, not years—reducing average wait times, publishing a transparency dashboard, and setting performance benchmarks that make citizens feel the change immediately.

FINAL THOUGHTS

The DMV has long been shorthand for bureaucratic frustration. But it doesn't have to be. By reimagining it as DMV 2.0—efficient, digital-first, and citizen-centered—we can prove that the government can deliver results where people actually live. If we can fix the DMV, we can restore trust in public service across California. Because when everyday government works, faith in the government returns. And when it works with fiduciary care, citizens know their time and money are being stewarded with respect. DMV 2.0 is more than convenience—it's a return on citizenship. By giving Californians back their time, we restore one of the most precious resources a government can protect: the daily lives of its people. If we fix the DMV, we fix trust in the California government.

CHAPTER 20

THE CLASSROOM CRISIS

RESTORING EDUCATION FOR THE NEXT GENERATION

For decades, California has prided itself on world-class universities, innovation hubs, and a spirit of discovery. But the truth is, our K–12 system is in crisis. Parents see classrooms overcrowded, teachers burned out, and students slipping through the cracks. For too many families, school is not the great equalizer—it's the great frustration. Education has become a partisan tug-of-war while kids sit in outdated classrooms with outcomes that no longer match California's promise.

Education is not an abstract issue—it's where California's future is being decided every single day. The way we fund, structure, and deliver education determines whether the next generation will thrive here or leave for opportunities elsewhere.

California spends among the highest amounts in the nation on education, yet its results lag behind those of other states. Test scores in reading and math remain stubbornly low. Families with means seek private options, while working families are left with fewer choices. Teachers often spend their own money on supplies, while administrative bloat grows. The system feels upside down.

Beyond academics, our kids are facing a mental health crisis, bullying, and digital distractions that schools are ill-equipped to handle. Parents feel left out of decision-making. Teachers feel unsupported. Students feel unseen.

A PERSONAL STORY

Now that my daughter is four years old and in transitional kindergarten (TK), she is experiencing her first public school setting after spending preschool in a co-op program. My wife carried much of the load in that co-op—organizing auctions, fundraising, and treating it almost like a second job—while I pitched in with woodworking and other projects. We chose a public school to lighten that burden, but we found a classroom with a higher student-to-teacher ratio. To cope, the school splits children into "early friends" and "late friends" groups, which overlap for part of the day, to avoid overwhelming the teacher. In her co-op, our daughter had close relationships with three teachers, whom she often spoke of warmly. That richness has been replaced by a far more crowded environment.

Ironically, even in public school, emails requesting volunteer hours arrive almost daily. What once was a bake sale and a plate of brownies has become a constant request for parental labor. The whole thing often feels less like a public school and more like a co-op without the intimacy. This experience underscores the larger problem: families are stretched thin, teachers are stretched thinner, and the system asks for more without giving more in return.

RESIDENCY MODEL FOR TEACHING

One of the most immediate ways to address California's classroom crisis is to rethink how we deploy the tens of thousands of people already training to become teachers. Today, the state has about 285,000 teachers of record serving 5.8 million public school students, leaving us with a student-to-teacher ratio of roughly 20 to 1—one of the highest in the nation. These numbers tell a simple story: our classrooms are overcrowded, and teachers are overwhelmed.

At the same time, California's universities are full of people actively working toward their teaching credentials. In the 2023–24 academic year, nearly 39,000 candidates were enrolled in teacher preparation programs across the state. Yet under the current structure, most of these students spend years moving through coursework, testing, and delayed student teaching before ever becoming a meaningful presence in a classroom. In medicine, we would never train doctors this way. We place medical students into hospitals early, allowing them to gain practical experience while providing immediate value. Our schools deserve the same residency-style model.

If every teaching candidate were given the opportunity to log their program hours by working directly in K–12 classrooms—screened, supervised, and supported by mentor teachers—the impact would be immediate and dramatic. Even accounting for the thousands of candidates already working as interns of record, we could instantly place more than 30,000 new instructional adults into schools. If they worked full time, the statewide student-to-adult ratio would fall from about 20.3 to 1 to 18.2 to 1, effectively reducing class load by two students per teacher. Even if these candidates worked half time, the ratio would improve to about 19.2 to 1. That's an 11–14 percent increase in staffing capacity, achieved without waiting years for new cohorts of graduates.

The real power of this approach is not just in lowering ratios but in reshaping the classroom experience itself. Imagine a third-grade class with not just one overburdened teacher, but two or three trained adults circulating—answering questions, pulling small groups for tutoring, and giving struggling students the one-on-one support they rarely get today. Instead of operating in survival mode, teachers could focus on instruction, knowing they had reliable, credential-bound colleagues at their side. For the candidates, the system would double as the best possible training ground: real children, real challenges, real mentorship. For schools, it would be a force multiplier—unlocking thousands of energetic, vetted, and motivated young educators waiting for their chance to serve.

This is the kind of fix we can flip on almost overnight. By reforming the credentialing pipeline into a true residency model, California could flood its schools with the most promising generation of teachers in decades—bright-eyed, fresh from college, and ready to lighten the load.

INFLATION/DEFLATION LENS

Educational failure is inflationary. When students graduate without skills, they earn less, spend less, and contribute less to the economy. Families pay out of pocket for tutoring or private options. Employers struggle to find qualified workers and pay more to train them. Everyone pays the cost of a broken pipeline.

Educational excellence is deflationary. A strong school system produces skilled workers, lowers unemployment, attracts businesses, and reduces crime. Every dollar invested in real outcomes multiplies across the economy—lowering social costs and raising productivity.

CALIFORNIA PATH

- **Residency Model for Teachers:** Reform the credentialing pipeline into a residency program, placing tens of thousands of credential candidates directly into classrooms as supervised support while they train.
- **Transparency for Parents:** Publish a clear, accessible dashboard showing school performance, budgets, and outcomes so families can make informed choices.
- **Career-Ready Pathways:** Expand vocational programs, apprenticeships, and partnerships with community colleges so students graduate with employable skills.
- **Mental Health Integration:** Normalize mental health support in schools by funding counselors, peer support programs, and crisis response teams.
- **Speed of Henderson Standards:** Implement reforms with urgency—reducing class sizes, delivering new technology, and clearing bureaucratic hurdles within months, not years.

FINAL THOUGHTS

California's future depends on classrooms that work. We cannot afford to let bureaucracy, politics, or inertia rob the next generation of opportunity. Education must once again be the ladder of mobility and the foundation of abundance. By restoring dignity to students, teachers, and parents, we can transform frustration into pride. As I observe my daughter's first steps in public school, I see both the challenges and the promise. Fixing our schools isn't just a policy choice—it's a moral obligation. A government that invests in classrooms at the Speed of Henderson honors its fiduciary duty to every California family.

CHAPTER 21

CALIFORNIA'S HEALTHCARE CROSSROADS

TOWARD ACCESS AND AFFORDABILITY

Healthcare in California is a paradox: if Washington falters, California must take control of its own health future—because waiting on DC has never been our path to progress. California is one of the most innovative states in the world, yet millions here still struggle with affordability, access, and trust in the system. As a small business owner, I've experienced this firsthand. With six employees, I rely on Covered California to provide health insurance. Without subsidies, our premiums would be unaffordable. Those subsidies—enhanced under the American Rescue Plan Act (ARPA) and the Inflation Reduction Act (IRA)—are set to expire at the end of 2025 unless Congress renews them. If they lapse, Californians face massive premium spikes, with hundreds of thousands at risk of losing coverage altogether.

I also know what it's like to navigate the health system personally. I've been a Kaiser Permanente member for years. Kaiser isn't loved by everyone—it still carries a stigma from its early days, and some dislike its health maintenance organization (HMO) model. But for me, Kaiser works. It's a one-stop shop where I can handle everything in one place, without crisscrossing town to see different doctors. That convenience matters when you're busy running a business and raising a family. It's good in some ways, limiting in others—but it highlights a core truth: California's healthcare feels like a patchwork, and the experience varies wildly depending on where you land.

I should also admit something that many people probably relate to: I really hate going to the doctor. I've been blessed with good health and excellent blood pressure at my age, and I usually only go in when I feel awful—like if I've come down with the flu or COVID-19. The last time I landed in the ER was years ago with diverticulitis, and that experience reminded me how vulnerable we all are when we put off proactive care. I know that regular health management is imperative, but like many people who know what to do with their money but don't actually follow through, I fall short. I know I should go to the doctor once a year for a checkup, but if I feel healthy, I often skip it, even though I know that isn't wise.

Kaiser once surprised me by mailing a colorectal cancer screening test. At first, I thought it was odd—having to administer something like that myself at home. But once I got past the initial reaction, I realized how convenient it was—no appointment, no drive across town, no waiting room. A couple of days later, the results arrived directly in my email. That small experience showed me what healthcare at scale could be: proactive, convenient, and efficient. Most individual physicians wouldn't think to mail out at-home screenings for people like me, who don't like going to the doctor. But a system designed for scale can—and that's what true innovation in healthcare should deliver.

As Governor of California, I would tap the best and the brightest from across the health sector and issue requests for proposals to bring forward the most effective ideas. That's what leadership means to me—empowering the best minds, not mandating one-size-fits-all bureaucracy. From telehealth to AI diagnostics to new payment models, we can knit together a cohesive plan based on data, not ideology. If the federal government insists on letting subsidies collapse, we must accept that reality and prepare. The wave of uninsured individuals is not something to wait for—it's something to confront with clear-eyed planning and bold reform.

Not everyone has been blessed with the excellent health I have enjoyed—and healthcare is also the story of those closest to me. One of my longtime and most trusted colleagues has been by my side through multiple companies over two decades. When her husband endured his third battle with cancer last year—a fight that stretched more than twelve months before ultimately taking his life—we were in the front row with her. It was brutal to watch: she was caring for her husband as his body failed piece by piece, managing her work, and trying to keep her own life afloat. On top of the heartbreak, her family faced the insanity of more than $1 million in healthcare bills for his treatments. That number is unthinkable: without insurance, most Americans would simply be priced out of the fight. A million dollars is about twenty years of net after-tax salaries for many families. Without coverage, the system essentially says your life isn't worth saving. That's not just broken policy—it's immoral.

THE NUMBERS THAT MATTER

Today, about 93–94 percent of Californians have some form of health coverage. That's progress, but it still leaves nearly 2.7 million uninsured. Roughly half of Californians receive insurance through employer-sponsored plans, while around 15 million rely on Medi-Cal. Medicare covers another 6.6 million people, and Covered California—the state's health exchange—serves about 1.98 million, nearly all of whom rely on subsidies to make premiums affordable. Less than 3 percent of purchases are made directly in the private market without subsidies.

Small businesses are especially vulnerable: only about half of them currently offer health benefits, and for those that do, the average family plan now costs over $25,000 a year, with employees paying about $6,300 out of pocket. For many owners, it's a choice between covering employees or keeping the doors open.

Looking forward to the next five years, California faces a dangerous convergence of problems. If the subsidy cliff is not addressed, as many as two million Californians could lose their coverage. Medi-Cal is already under strain as budgets groan under expanded eligibility and rising pharmaceutical costs, and shortfalls could worsen. In rural counties, primary care shortages force residents to drive hours for basic treatment, a reality that will deepen as the physician workforce ages.

PHARMACEUTICALS, NUTRACEUTICALS, AND FIDUCIARY DUTY

The pharmaceutical and nutraceutical industries reveal a larger truth: when oversight fails, Californians pay the price—financially and physically. They are two sides of the same coin: industries where unfettered profiteering has run rampant.

People are overmedicated, often without their doctors even knowing the full panel of substances they are taking. Over-the-counter supplements can interact with prescription drugs in dangerous ways, yet there is no systematic process to track them. At the very least, this creates financial harm as families spend enormous sums chasing lifestyle promises; at worst, it creates real physical harm.

As a financial advisor, I would never make recommendations without seeing the full financial picture. Yet doctors are expected to prescribe without knowing the full medical picture of what their patients are consuming. That disconnect is unacceptable. Bringing balance back to these markets—through transparency, regulation, and integration of patient information—is essential to both safety and affordability.

EMDR: A NONDRUG PATH FOR TRAUMA

Another area where California can lead is in expanding awareness and access to EMDR—eye movement desensitization and reprocessing therapy. My mother, a licensed marriage and family therapist, has been using this approach with patients for decades. EMDR is a nondrug, noninvasive treatment for trauma and post-traumatic stress disorder. It works by mimicking the rapid eye movement of sleep, helping the brain properly file away traumatic memories that otherwise remain unresolved and disruptive.

For many veterans and survivors of trauma, EMDR has proven to be life-changing—offering relief without the side effects or dependency risks of pharmaceuticals. Yet despite multiple levels of certification and decades of practice, EMDR remains underfunded, under-taught, and largely unknown in the broader healthcare system. The reason is simple: drug companies have lobbyists, and therapies without a profit engine struggle to gain traction.

California should invest in training, research, and coverage for therapies like EMDR. Doing so would save lives, reduce reliance on medication, and provide veterans and trauma survivors with the care they deserve.

A FIDUCIARY APPROACH TO HEALTHCARE

As a fiduciary advisor, I see healthcare similarly to portfolio management: accountability, transparency, and alignment with the client's goals are crucial. Right now, California's healthcare system fails that test. Patients—the clients—bear the costs while executives reap the profits. We need a system that treats Californians' health as an investment, not an expense.

That means demanding transparency in pricing. It means reining in middlemen who drive up drug and insurance costs without adding value. It means measuring success not by hospital revenues but by patient outcomes. And it means seeing every policy choice through the fiduciary ethic: does this serve the people first, or does it serve entrenched interests?

California doesn't need to reinvent healthcare from scratch, but we do need bold reforms. We must expand access by building on Medi-Cal while offering affordable, streamlined public options for middle-income families stuck in the gap. We can leverage California's innovation engine—from biotech to telemedicine—to reduce costs and expand reach, especially in rural areas. The state should also use its scale for bargaining power, negotiating lower drug prices and insurance premiums the way other nations already do. At the same time, we must reduce administrative waste by modernizing billing and digitizing systems, freeing up resources for direct care. Finally, we need to invest in prevention and mental health, recognizing that every dollar spent on wellness reduces costs downstream.

INFLATION/DEFLATION LENS

Runaway healthcare costs are inflationary. Every dollar a family spends on premiums or medical debt is a dollar not spent on housing, education, or local businesses. Employers, too, are burdened with higher costs, reducing their ability to hire and grow. The looming subsidy cliff after 2025 could raise premiums by 66 percent for nearly two million Californians, adding billions of dollars in additional household costs and squeezing small businesses that already struggle to offer coverage.

Affordable, transparent care is deflationary. When preventive care is accessible, chronic conditions cost less to manage. When drug prices are negotiated fairly, family budgets stretch further. When administrative waste is cut, dollars flow back into wages, innovation, and community health. Avoiding the subsidy cliff, strengthening Medi-Cal, and expanding access through a public option would immediately stabilize costs and protect both families and employers. Healthcare done right isn't just compassionate—it's economically stabilizing. And just as a fiduciary protects clients from undue risk, California must protect families and small businesses from systemic financial harm caused by runaway health costs and subsidy cliffs.

CALIFORNIA PATH

- **Fiduciary Duty in Care:** Require all reforms to meet a fiduciary test—transparency, accountability, and proof that Californians receive value for every healthcare dollar spent.
- **Public Option Expansion:** Create a streamlined California

public health plan for families who don't qualify for Medi-Cal but can't afford private insurance.
- **Biotech for All:** Partner with the University of California and California State University systems to deploy biotech breakthroughs—especially in telemedicine and diagnostics—directly into public clinics.
- **Drug Price Negotiation:** Use California's size to negotiate lower prescription drug prices statewide.
- **Nondrug Therapies:** Expand support and coverage for EMDR and other nondrug, noninvasive, low-cost, high-impact treatments that can be deployed immediately at the state level.

FINAL THOUGHTS

California stands at a healthcare crossroads, and as Governor, I intend to build a state rooted in Independence, innovation, and trust. We can continue down a path of rising costs, unequal access, and frustration, or we can build a system guided by fiduciary duty and respect for every patient. Access to affordable care is not a luxury—it is the foundation of dignity and abundance. I know this not just from data but from my own experience navigating Kaiser, from my reliance on Covered California to cover employees, and from watching a trusted colleague's family face a million-dollar battle with cancer. These stories—personal and shared—are why reform cannot wait. We can transform California's healthcare from a liability into a model for the nation, proving once again that when the government answers only to the people, it delivers results that matter most. California can once again lead the nation—not by accepting broken systems, but by proving that healthcare can be abundant, affordable, and accountable. That's not just policy—it's leadership rooted in Independence and accountability.

CHAPTER 22

A TRUE MERITOCRACY

THE CITIZEN STATUS CARD

I believe merit should matter again—not wealth, not connections, not manipulation, but rather effort, service, and contribution. A society thrives when those who give more of themselves to the community also receive more opportunity, dignity, and recognition. In a true meritocracy, everyone has a path to rise—and nobody is left without a reason to try.

For decades, the red and the blue have been pitted against each other by external forces—media algorithms, partisan donors, and bad actors who profit from keeping Americans divided. But when people come together to do tangible work for their communities, they rediscover something powerful: that we are far more alike than we are different. Working side by side—cleaning a park, helping a neighbor, mentoring a student—reminds us that human connection is our greatest strength. The Citizen Status Card would provide a framework to foster that belonging, helping Californians replace political division with shared purpose and pride.

We live in a time when millions feel untethered—starved for purpose, unsure of their place, and surrounded by institutions they no longer trust. Role models have faded, and too many drift with nothing to strive for beyond a paycheck or a screen. Meanwhile, communities are hurting, and those who want to help often don't know where to begin.

The Citizen Status Card proposal gives them a path—a gamelike, rewarding way to reengage with civic life and build pride through positive action. Here's the truth: nobody likes being labeled. But everyone loves being ranked—especially when it's for doing good.

The more you pitch in, the more you get out. From military service to paying your full tax bill on time—this is the point system we deserve.

The Citizen Status Card would make this real: a rewards program for being a solid, engaged citizen. It would offer discounts at participating businesses, priority access to public resources, and other tangible benefits that increase with your contributions. Participation would be voluntary, transparent, and protected under the California Consumer Privacy Act. No data sold. No pressure. Just contribution that earns reward.

Unlike credit card rewards programs, it would cost nothing to join. Instead, you would earn your way up the ranks through modern merit badges, tracked digitally in a clean, gamelike app. Each action checked off becomes a point of pride: "Look what I've done for my community." All data would be stored on the California blockchain—the same infrastructure we'll eventually use for voting. Before that, it could host anonymous public votes on policy, giving a real sense of where Californians stand, free from spin and algorithms.

California's promise has always been opportunity—and that opportunity must come from personal input. But in practice, opportunity has become too dependent on luck, connections, or where you start in life. Meritocracy—the idea that talent and effort should be rewarded—is slipping away. It's time to restore it with a tool that puts every Californian on a level playing field: the Citizen Status Card.

Today, Californians give much to the state but rarely feel they get much back. Taxes are high, but services feel strained. Too often, hard work doesn't translate into visible rewards, and good citizenship isn't recognized at all. Meanwhile, systems of credit, education, and employment increasingly reward based on who you know, not what you contribute. Many Californians—especially younger generations—feel that the social contract is broken.

As a fiduciary, I see it differently. Every citizen is an investor in California, contributing through their taxes, their labor, and their civic participation. But unlike private-sector investors, they don't get a clear return. That's not fair. And it's not sustainable. Californians deserve Independence from a system that only rewards insiders, not contributors—and from overreliance on distant federal or corporate interests that often dictate outcomes from afar. True Independence means Californians taking ownership of their own destiny, community by community.

THE CITIZEN STATUS CARD: TURNING CONTRIBUTION INTO CREDIT

The Citizen Status Card would function as a return on citizenship, tracking and rewarding contributions Californians make to the state and their communities. This isn't another ID card—it's a ledger of earned value and Independence in action.

It would recognize a wide range of contributions: serving in the military or Peace Corps, paying your full tax bill on time, volunteering for wildfire recovery or disaster relief, donating blood or registering as an organ donor, finishing school, or taking on community service roles like election volunteering, graffiti cleanup, grocery delivery for seniors, tutoring, mentorship, neighborhood watch, tree planting, literacy drives, or even pitching in on Gonzo Box shifts. Everyday responsibilities and acts of service would become modern badges of honor, building a record of effort and contribution that Californians could point to with pride. Each of these actions would earn points on the card, turning everyday responsibility and service into measurable credit. In a time when too many people are polarized behind screens, doomscrolling during their downtime, this system would give Californians something better to reach for—productive goals rooted in real-world contribution rather than online division. Instead of feeding cynicism, it would create momentum toward community and self-determination.

GAMIFYING CITIZENSHIP WITH THE META

The Citizen Status Card would also embrace design lessons from the gaming world. Imagine an app with bright visuals, satisfying sounds, and instant feedback—all the dopamine hits of a jackpot, but tied to doing good. With churches, civic groups, and traditional role models in decline, this digital merit system could fill that gap, making civic pride as engaging as any game—and fostering Independence through voluntary participation rather than mandates.

In gaming, META stands for "most effective tactic available." I learned this while playing games like *World of Warcraft* and *Overwatch*, where players must adapt or lose. The same is true in life and politics. Too often, leaders cling to outdated positions instead of applying the most effective tactic for today's reality. This point system is a META move—dynamic, evolving, responsive. Daily, weekly, and monthly challenges would keep participants engaged. Instead of collecting skins or coins, you'd collect civic experience points (XP) and public standing. Achievements could even be minted as non-fungible tokens (NFTs)—costing little to produce but offering unique proof of contribution.

REWARD PACKAGES

Participants could gain perks that make everyday life easier by gaining XP. Sample packages might include commuter perks like toll-free express lanes, bridge fee waivers, or free transit passes; outdoor adventure perks like free state park entry, early campground booking, or discounted gear rentals; and quality-of-life perks like museum access, farmers' market credits, childcare rebates, or wellness stipends. These are just examples—the public would vote on which rewards matter most.

INFLATION/DEFLATION LENS

A society that stops rewarding contributions is inflationary. When effort goes unrecognized, motivation fades, civic participation drops, and dependency grows. The government spends more to manage apathy—through subsidies, enforcement, and programs that try to buy back engagement. The result is higher costs, lower trust, and an inflated social deficit where people feel their work no longer matters.

The Citizen Status Card is deflationary. It channels personal effort into measurable value, turning goodwill into real savings for both citizens and the state. Every act of service—volunteering, paying taxes, mentoring, helping a neighbor—reduces the need for bureaucracy and strengthens shared ownership.

Incentivized contribution restores pride, lowers waste, and rebalances the social contract. When people see clear returns on good citizenship, inflation of cynicism gives way to deflation of cost—and abundance takes its place.

CALIFORNIA PATH

- **Launch the Citizen Status Card:** Build a secure, blockchain-backed platform that tracks contributions while protecting privacy.
- **Gamify Civic Engagement:** Design the platform with gaming-style feedback—bright visuals, challenges, and civic XP—to make participation engaging and addictive in a healthy way.
- **Reward Civic Participation:** Tie benefits—fee reductions, tuition credits, and grant eligibility—to points earned.
- **Integrate Across Agencies:** Ensure that every state system—from the DMV to CalTrans to the UC system—accepts points as part of eligibility and benefit structures.
- **Transparency and Trust:** Publish an anonymized dashboard so Californians can see how points are earned and redeemed, creating visible accountability.

FINAL THOUGHTS

California's future depends on restoring fairness and Independence, and rewarding effort. The Citizen Status Card offers a modern social contract that turns everyday contributions into real opportunities. By gamifying civic engagement and making effort the true currency of advancement, California can once again prove that when we work together—free from dependency on Washington or Wall Street—we rise together.

CLOSING

ABUNDANT CALIFORNIA, ABUNDANT NATION

America today feels like a nation stuck on a psychiatrist's couch. The two dominant political parties have become caricatures of Freud's most infamous constructs.

The Republican Party has become the id—pure impulse, chasing gratification at all costs: cut taxes now, build walls now, own the libs now. Long-term consequences? Who cares? The id doesn't plan. It reacts. It rages.

The Democratic Party has become the superego—the moral perfectionist with a savior complex. It seeks justice, fairness, and equity—noble goals, no doubt—but often in ways disconnected from everyday reality. The superego pushes purity over pragmatism, even when it alienates the very people it claims to fight for.

What we desperately lack is the ego—the balancing force, the rational, grounded adult in the room, not driven by desire or guilt but by results. That's what Independence in California must represent: the steadying force that integrates passion with practicality and ideals with outcomes. This is not about splitting the difference or compromising for the sake of compromise. It's about integration—taking the raw passion of the id and the noble aspirations of the superego and channeling them into something that actually works.

For most of my life, balance has been my obsession. As a financial advisor, balance is what I help clients pursue—the sweet spot between saving and enjoying life, risk and reward. As a husband and father, it's the struggle between professional ambition and cherished family moments. As a pilot, I know balance isn't a luxury—it's survival. And as an American, I've realized that balance isn't just missing from our politics—it's actively under attack. We've become a nation addicted to extremes—amplified by media narratives, tribal politicians, influential algorithms, and social media echo chambers. But when everything is an emergency, nothing truly gets solved. The solution isn't to veer harder to the left or to double down on the right. It's to do what every thoughtful American knows we need to do: recenter, rebalance, and rebuild.

After almost twenty years at Merrill Lynch, I decided to walk away from a successful career that had defined much of my adult life. I had built deep relationships, achieved milestones, and worked with incredible clients—but I also felt constrained. The system, while powerful, had grown rigid and risk-averse in my view, prioritizing the institution over the individual. I realized that to operate at my highest level—to innovate, to challenge convention, to truly serve people with Independence of thought—I needed to step away and build something of my own. Leaving wasn't easy. It was a leap into uncertainty. But it was also the most liberating decision of my professional life. That leap gave birth to Echo45 Advisors, and with it, a new understanding of what Independence really means.

I now feel that way about California. For our state to function at its highest level, it too must reclaim its Independence—Independence from party dictates, corporate capture, and bureaucratic inertia. California has all the raw talent, creativity, and wealth needed to thrive, but like any great professional trapped in a system that no longer serves them, it must choose to chart its own course. Only through independent leadership can we unleash the full potential of this state and the people who call it home.

This conviction is why I believe we need a new political home—a set of values rooted deeply in logic, fairness, financial discipline, community service, technology, and above all, balance. We need leadership that listens instead of shouting, leads instead of blaming, and governs instead of playing games. This book isn't radical; it's radically sensible. It's a call to action for every American who feels politically homeless—the 80 percent of us who are tired of performative nonsense and are desperate to return to basic decency: honesty, hard work, fairness, and yes—balance.

This book has been about reclaiming the promise of California through Independence, balance, and abundance. Across these chapters, I have shared stories from my own life and from the people I serve—stories of frustration with broken systems but also of hope, ingenuity, and resilience. Each policy, each reform, and each idea presented here is not theory—it is a step in a master plan to prove that the government can still work and that California can still lead.

The choice before us is clear. We can continue to drift, allowing polarization, bureaucracy, and inertia to sap our strength. Or we can choose to act with urgency—to govern at the Speed of Henderson, to bring a fiduciary ethic to public service, and to demand a return on citizenship for every Californian. That is how we restore trust, rebuild dignity, and create opportunity.

I believe deeply that when Californians come together to build—not just to argue, not just to point fingers, but to actually build—we rediscover respect where contempt once lived. We find common cause in solving problems that affect us all: wildfires, homelessness, healthcare, housing, education, safety. Every time we notch a win together, we prove to ourselves and the nation that progress is possible.

California can be proudly purple—neither blue nor red, but a blend that honors our diversity of thought and experience. That is our strength. Proud Purple means taking the best ideas from all sides, discarding the extremes, and focusing on what works. It means the government answering only to the people, not to parties or special interests. It means making California a place worth fighting for, worth staying in, and worth passing on to our children.

If California leads with Independence and abundance, the nation will follow. That is our responsibility and our opportunity. Together, we can turn the page from scarcity to abundance, from contempt to respect, from drift to momentum. Together, we can build an abundant California—and in doing so, spark an abundant nation.

Thank you for joining me on this journey. I'm not a career politician—I'm an executive, an advisor, a husband, a father, and above all, someone who loves people deeply. Californians, Americans, and people everywhere—I believe we all have the power to help each other if we can just clear the noise. Balance is not weakness. Balance is strength. And it's how we move forward—together.

CALIFORNIA 2.0!

If you are excited about the vision I've outlined here—especially the urgency of ending homelessness and wildfires as California's top priorities—then I ask for your vote in the 2026 gubernatorial election. Please join my candidacy, spread the word, and help build a California that rewards Independence, balance, and abundance. A vote for Jon Henderson is a vote for an independent free-thinker not bound by party talking points or corporate donor limitations. It is also a vote to meet California's top needs with a growth mindset instead of a scarcity mentality—tackling challenges like homelessness and wildfires with optimism, innovation, and resolve.

www.ingramcontent.com/pod-product-compliance
Lightning Source LLC
Chambersburg PA
CBHW031152020426
42333CB00013B/632